Carry This? Up That?!

Hiking The Appalachian Trail With No Hair Dryer

SANDY WALLACE

DEDICATION

*For all women ....of all ages. May you climb all of your
"mountains" ....while you can.*

Edited by:
Nancy Hoover
Janice Vitale
Elaine MacDonald

This is a work of *mostly* non-fiction. There is a *little* exaggeration and some names have been changed.

TABLE OF CONTENTS

Prologue

"Jule, do you think we'll actually see any rattlesnakes? Plus, I was thinking, does bear mace really work like it says it does? Maybe we should have gotten some just to be on the safe side. And what about toilet paper? I hate to add extra weight. We could just wipe with leaves," I rambled on to my bestie as we stumbled along an especially rocky section of the Appalachian Trail in Pennsylvania.

"I don't know about the snakes or bear mace, but yeah, I am bringing toilet paper. I'm not wiping with leaves. Sandy, you worry way too much," answered Julie.

"Yeah, I guess maybe I do. I just like to always be ready, you know? I want to always have a plan B just in case something bad happens," I said.

"Maybe you'd feel better if you relaxed and enjoyed what was happening instead of trying to figure it all out," countered Julie.

She nailed it. That was totally what I needed to do. I really, really wanted to be "in the moment." I just found it extremely difficult to do. Maybe, just maybe, this brief but already spectaccular trek on the AT would help me to achieve this. I was sure going to try.

Chapter 1: Why hike?

Julie told me at the end of the Appalachian Trail trip, she felt that she had lost her soul, and hoped that the solace and peace of the woods would help her to find it again.

In her words: "Once upon a time there was a lady who lost her soul. She became friends with a man through his blog that chronicled his hike on the AT. Although they never met in person, she knew he had gained something very sacred from his AT journey. He encouraged and reassured her this was something she could do and repeatedly told her how strong, smart, and courageous she was. She was in the middle of a second divorce and needed to feel peace and joy again. She wanted her soul back. She had never hiked or backpacked but listened to his every word and started making a plan.

On June 30th, 2016 she went to Harpers Ferry, West Virginia with all her hiking gear and started heading north. She endured blisters, a sprain, pulled muscles, bruises, thunder and lightning storms on a mountain ridge, snakes, bears, rocks, and heat but wanted to push on. The trail was healing her soul one step at a time. She experienced random acts of kindness, trail magic, and raw emotions. New friends appeared daily, and she was healing. Slowly she realized she could trust her common sense, gut instincts, and decisions. Nature cleansed her. She discovered how strong she was mentally, emotionally, and physically. On August 6th, 2016 she had hiked thirty-eight days and covered 342.3 miles taking her to the border of New York and New Jersey. Sitting on the rock marking that border she realized her soul was always there. She just needed to open her eyes and take one step at a time." Julie said that the trip allowed her to do that.

For me, there was a parallel search, but it started before the trip, and it was my spirit that had disappeared. It started when she told me that she didn't recognize *me* anymore. She wondered where I had gone and when this old woman had appeared. I wondered that as well. I didn't really want to check into the "shady pines" of my life. I guess I just lost confidence that I could still "git er done." It seems Julie did find her soul on the trail. I found my spirit when I agreed to step onto it.

We hiked for different reasons. Me, to find my lost spirit. Julie, to find her lost soul. I would like to think we were both successful in our own way, on our own journeys, that so often had intersected during the nearly four decades of friendship we have shared.

A woman can have several different best friends over a lifetime. Maybe she maintains a single girlfriend from early childhood on up to dementia, the nursing home, or death, whatever comes first. Or maybe the best friends fit into different categories, like one for work and one for social activities.

In my own case, I have had several throughout my almost sixty-two years. My first bestie lasted from first grade to junior high. From seventh grade until graduation, I had several best friends. In college, there were my roommates. I am still in contact with all of these women, although I am much closer today to some than to others. As an adult, I have also had multiple best friends over the years. I have had different, wonderful experiences with all of the best friends I have ever had. But in all of my time, I have only had one "adventure bestie." There has been one woman to whom I have always been able to say, "Hey, do you want to......?" And she is always up for it.

She is a why-not kinda girl. Although we share many interests, have similar warped humor, can be quick witted when we need to be, are nearly age mates (I am the elder by two years) and have both always faced adversity with a step forward and a positive attitude, in many respects, we couldn't be more different.

I am a crazy animal loving, mostly vegetarian who volunteers at SPCAs, struggling with each departure to not take yet one more animal into my home. Julie is herself an animal lover, but is just a little more rational about them. Plus, she hunts. And fishes. A big, fat, YUCK to both. I am an avid reader, have strong political views, and play a good number of musical instruments with fair to marginal success. Julie has an amazing talent for woodworking, actually making things that come out with the corners squared, can fix stuff, and has excellent taste when it comes to interior décor-ating. Those are not my strong suits. In fact, I don't think I actu-ally carry a card in those suits at all. She dresses fashionably, al-ways looks classy, and wears the appropriate amount of makeup. I am extremely casual, don't own foundation, but do admit occa-sionally, and I do mean occasionally, to applying lipstick. Her man-picker gene has not always functioned adequately, but then mine has been somewhat defective as well. I certainly can't judge here.

Regarding our homes, it is what you might imagine. Her rustic home is suited to be photographed for a magazine and in fact was featured in Log Cabin. She mows acres, stocks a pond with bass and bluegills, and has a wrap-around porch that is home to original Amish furniture, some of which she was given for de-livering their babies. My house? Well, it's nice. Especially from the outside, where it, too, is very rustic. It's sided with board and batten, again from the local Amish. However, there was no birth-ing process that directly involved me when obtaining our lumber. We just bought it outright. Cash deal.

However, as I recall, one of the Amish gentleman that my husband, John, was dealing with did have a very pregnant wife. She would soon be delivering their seventh child, and young Daniel was understandably nervous because they were currently without a midwife. The more John talked with Daniel regarding our lumber deal, the more often their conversation digressed into the topic of the impending new baby that likely Daniel would be delivering. This apparently was terrifying for him.

Now, my husband is a problem solver, and a very good one. So am I. We often make a very excellent tag team when it comes to gnarly situations. I am not sure at what point Julie's name came up as a possible Amish midwife stand-in. But, it did, and before the last load of lumber was piled in front of our house, Julie had delivered her first Amish baby.

I recently purchased a riding lawn mower, much to my husband's dismay, because he didn't think we needed one. We did. I suspect we mow roughly an acre. Rough is the operative word here. We mow weeds. Precious little grass sprouts up. We plant grass, but it is the weeds that grow.

To say my house is tastefully decorated on the inside would be a big, fat lie. Nothing matches. If shabby chic is considered to be in vogue, then I suppose I do make that cut. I have a couple family antiques spattered in among my rummage sale finds, of which there are many. There is no theme. Well, I take that back. There is a sort of nautical thing going on, because we own a sailboat, and have a few nautical items. There is also a bit of Africa with the relics John has brought back from when he worked in Sudan and Rwanda. I don't know if sailing and Africa actually constitute a true theme. There is no order. There is a lot of mismatched stuff. I do love my home, though. I am most definitely not a fine wine kind of person when it comes to interior decorating. I am totally cheap beer.

Julie's home, in stark contrast, is of course just as tasteful inside as out. Her theme is western. There is order. There is quality. And, there is a room designated primarily to house her collection of cowboy boots. I kid you not. I have seen this. Can I just say, never in my life, have I seen so many cowboy boots in one place. There are racks and racks. All full. All tasteful. Me? I have an abundant supply of flip flops. But, you know what? We are totally OK with our stuff. She, with her western décor, me with my junk. I don't want her place, she doesn't want mine. We just want to have adventures together. We want to make fun memories.

And at this point in life, Julie would also like to meet a pleasant, kind, dependable man with a tractor who can fix stuff.

Cooking would be nice, as well as liking to hunt and fish. Or, at least eat the venison and fish she brings home. At this point in my life, I can honestly say that I am fortunate enough to be partnered up with and married to an amazing man. He is compassionate, kind, occasionally punctual, and makes me laugh; always. He brings out the best in me. I can say without hesitation that my time with him just keeps getting richer. Plus, he is handsome in a disheveled way. At least, I think so. That's what counts, right?

Julie and I met back in 1981 when she came to work at Corning Hospital, which incidentally, has just been leveled and where I worked for ten years. My daughter was born there, my husband had three surgeries and recovered from his near death bout of sepsis just a couple of years ago. So very bitter sweet. So very many memories there.

We were in our twenties, young wives, young mothers, registered nurses, and as all young people, just trying to figure out how to keep our lives on track and raise nice kids. We were hopeful, idealistic, and filled with the seemingly endless enthusiasm of youth. We shared the good times and the bad in both our professional and our personal lives. We cried through our subsequent divorces, encouraged each other when we entered back into the dating world, shared in the struggles of our kids, and waded through the murky waters that were too often our lives. We have worked at being good people, strong women, and tried very hard to never say, "I can't do that."

Being OB/GYN (obstetrical and gynecological) nurses, we certainly had our share of excitement with life and death situations. Julie was a great labor nurse and has delivered many babies over the years. When a nurse delivers the baby, it generally isn't by choice. It's because the obstetrician or midwife was late. Too late. In all my time, I only caught one baby. I can't count Julie's catches, and likely, neither can she. And starting with Daniel, there have been a few Amish neighbors thrown into her war chest because they would come for her when their own midwife wasn't going to make it. Clearly, we had our work challenges as well as our activity adventures.

There are so very many labor and delivery stories that it would take yet another book to describe them with the detail they deserve. Suffice it to say, the most horrific one for me was the time I was pushing a stretcher to the operating room, along with several other nurses, for an emergency Cesarean section. Julie was riding on the stretcher with the patient, her pointer and middle fingers inserted into the patient's vagina, trying to push the baby's head off the umbilical cord. The medical term is prolapsed cord, and it is a life and death emergency.

If the baby is delivered vaginally, it will likely be stillborn. Julie kept calling out that the heart-rate was dropping. We had to get that baby out. So many of my memories of the ten years I spent working in the OB-GYN unit have either been forgotten or blurred in together. Not this event. It remains isolated on its very own shelf in the library of my mind and is as vivid as if it happened yesterday.

Arriving in the operating room, I stepped aside, watching as Julie was draped in the sterile field along with the patient. At this point she could not move her hand from the cord. She was still announcing the ever decreasing heart rate. The baby was in distress. The on-call anesthesiologist had not yet arrived. Nothing would be happening until he got there.

I returned to the nursery to ready all of the available equipment for what we called a "bad baby." Those were the newborns who were not thriving. They were compromised either from the delivery itself or some underlying condition. I still remember working on that baby, who really never had a chance. He was dead when we got him in the nursery, but still, you try. I remember the tears of the nurses, the parents, and yes, the doctors. Losing any patient is tough enough, losing a perfectly healthy baby is the worst. Julie and I don't talk about that particular delivery very much. Better to remember and discuss the fun times than the tragedies. Way less stressful to recall the garden hose douche and the bounty hunter.

Yes. We actually did have a patient whose husband shared quite enthusiastically, the process of douching his wife with a garden hose, and telling us how it made her giggle. Yeah. Really. I could not make this stuff up. We also had ourselves a real, live bounty hunter waiting patiently in the labor and delivery suite for a criminal in the birthing room to become a dad. We all thought that was indeed considerate of the guy. Plus, he was just a little on the hot side. OK. He was really very hot.

We get along well and have often joked that it ain't every girl-friend you can pee in the woods with! We have run relay races, marathons, completed triathlons, biked across the northeast, around lakes, and also the Gaspe Peninsula in Quebec.

For all of these adventures, it has mostly been me who has asked, "Hey, do you want to…….?"

Recently, very recently, Julie asked me. "Sandy, do you want to hike on the Appalachian Trail?"

Yup. She blindsided me. I was feeling my age. I wasn't looking for new adventures. I was into doing damage control to the body I had abused. Suddenly it was me who was being asked, "Why not?" I am not proud of my response. I am ashamed to say that I said, "I can't." I broke our *why not* rule with that answer.

I would like to be reporting on my extremely positive, can-do, optimistic, love-a-challenge attitude. I would like to say without reservation, that my enthusiasm and behavior toward my bestie's idea of the Appalachian Trail hike was nothing short of totally supportive. It. Was. Not. Looking back, I have to say, I was pretty much a dumb ass, mixed with equal parts Debbie Downer and Patty Pathetic. Yes. Me. Miss Think-Outside-the-Box, always up for an adventure, had turned into an elderly doom and gloom cloud. WTF.

I am not quite sure at what point I decided that I was old. Maybe it was looking at my very sun damaged, wrinkly skin that stared back at me when I looked in the mirror or down at my forearms. Maybe it was the generally unkempt mop of gray-white hair that adorned my head or the sagging skin around my knees that made my legs look scarily like a soup chicken. But then again, I did have a health scare several years ago when I tried snow-blowing our driveway uphill, and I got the thing stuck. I tugged, yanked, and pushed like a crazy woman to move that monster from the ditch I drove it into.

The extreme exhaustion I pushed myself to that day kicked up a heart arrhythmia that sent me to the cardiologist for a full work-up. Miraculously, I didn't suffer any permanent damage, but the episode certainly caught my attention. I simply could not physically do those tasks that once came so easily. I became tired. I got hurt. I got sore. So. Big deal. I was not twenty-five anymore. I wasn't thirty-five, forty-five, or fifty-five. I was sixty-one years old. I had arrived at the seventh decade of my life. I was definitely over halfway to the finish line. However, instead of aging like a classy broad, I decided that I was old. Shit. My husband, who was twenty years my senior, seemed younger that I did. Sadly, I was old beyond my years. Clearly, I was not handling the cumulative effect that the years were having upon me very well. Not even a little bit well.

My husband was not at all helpful with this aging thing, either. Once upon a time, back in the days when I still colored my hair, people would often mistake me for his daughter. Not anymore. In fact, we are generally considered to be age mates. Nice for him. Sucks for me. Recently we had an opportunity to save money on some admission tickets. If I were sixty-five, I would only pay half the fare.

Without any hesitation, John said, "You might as well say you're sixty-five, you look it. They won't question you." Really? Really??

It was no wonder I started to believe I was old. Add my recent lower back pain problems, my obviously arthritic hands, and my often tender knees; yeah, I was old. My years of athleticism had come to a pitiful, painful, and seemingly abrupt end. I couldn't run or jog because of my joints. I didn't dare push my heart rate up very far for fear of re-capturing the arrhythmia, and a retirement community was starting to sound like a good idea. The ultimate insult was when folks at my mother's assisted living home asked when I was moving in and began talking with me about the food and activities. Shit. I was doomed. Old way before my time and heading down the hill of life like an out of control bobsled. One of the old, rickety wooden types.

"I can't do that. Damn. No, really. I just can't. I mean I really want to! It sounds amazing! What an adventure! I just can't manage carrying all that weight. You know how my back isn't so good. I've had problems the last couple of years. Remember when I was telling you about going to physical therapy and all? Doing those core strengthening exercises and taking the anti-inflammatory and muscle relaxing meds? I sure don't want to have surgery, so I'm pretty much in the damage control mode. I really, really wish I could, though. I think it's a great idea for an adventure. You'll have such a good time," I rambled on and on with my litany of excuses. And I didn't stop.

"You know we have the boat, too. I hate to take off much time from the summer. Plus, we already have some commitments. You know those family obligations you just can't get out of. You sure know how that goes. And then there's my mom. I can't not be available for more than a couple of days. And my cats. I just love those kitties to death, and I hate to ask John to take on that responsibility. I mean, he would, but he just doesn't appreciate them the way I do. He has our little wiener dog to take care of already. Oh yeah, I almost forgot. There's the garden and lawn that need attention. I bought that riding lawn mower, and John doesn't know how to use it. I'm just not comfortable leaving all that work for him. He doesn't eat right when I'm gone, either. I'd feel guilty if I went away, and he got sick," I droned on and on and on. I was totally on a roll.

"And then there's my hips and knees. Did I mention I've been having some issues with my right hip and knee? It's the leg I broke back when I was twelve. Likely arthritis, but still, I don't want to over use them and get an injury. I'm having enough trouble with my back. I mean, you know, I really, really, really would like to go with you. You'll have such a great time! I'll miss seeing all of the wildlife. You'll probably get some great pictures. Maybe you'll even see a bear! Or a rattlesnake! That would be so cool! I wouldn't mind the spiders and all the bugs but would worry about Lyme disease. Have you thought of that? But I do think it's cool you want to do this."

I concluded my seemingly endless list of reasons, or if I were to be honest with myself, excuses; why I could not possibly hike part of the Appalachian Trail with my biking, running, and adventure seeking bestie.

Additional reasons (excuses) that I didn't share with her were: sleeping on the teensy mattress pad, stinging insects, bears, skunks, porcupines, raccoons, snakes, rain, cold, heat, potential for injury, stinking because you can't shower, lack of good food because fruits and vegetables are too heavy to carry, and lugging all that weight up and down mountains. It wasn't that I didn't enjoy a good adventure now and then, it was just that I felt I had reached the point in my life where I enjoyed amenities.

Sure. I loved wildlife. But mostly, I loved the creatures in the wild, not in my tent. Speaking of tents, I had camped a great deal over the years. It was fun. *Was* is the operative word here. Today my idea of camping was more about being up and off the ground, in one of those RV's. Yes. I had become complacent. I had become soft. I went to the YMCA every day, but didn't actually perspire very much. I mean I did sometimes get my heart rate up over one hundred, but just barely. I never got out of breath.

Looking back, I realize I didn't actually articulate all of my reasons, or as I really should call them, excuses. I know I can ramble on at times, but when Julie first mentioned the idea to me, I didn't have an arsenal of responses or reasons not to go. My initial answer was something like, "That's a great idea, but I could never do it because of my back. I mean I could never carry a pack."

I gradually expanded on explanations of why I couldn't possibly do this. Also, at first, I didn't actually take her seriously. I thought she was just sort of thinking out loud about what a cool adventure it could be. I didn't think she was actually going to hike through the woods. Alone. Spending weeks at a time without applying makeup and prancing around in her cowboy boots.

This is the woman who insisted on packing a hair dryer and dress sandals in the saddlebag of her bike on our first big biking trip. I never understood why she would add all of that extra weight when she crammed her short hair into a helmet for the better part of the day. We would check into a motel, shower, walk to the closest place to eat, which was usually not very classy, and then collapse into bed. Who needed good hair? And those clunky sandals? Really? Where did they belong on our bike trip? Then, there is the makeup. This girl ALWAYS wears makeup, dangly earrings, additional assorted jewelry, and a well-planned ensemble.

Me? I am extremely casual. Actually, I just look like shit most of the time. Gym shorts or sweat pants, dark colored t-shirts so I don't need a bra (not that I need one anyway), scraggly gray-white hair, no jewelry except the skinny gold chain around my neck and opal ring that serves as both engagement and wedding band, and flip flops or sneakers, depending upon the season. Clean I was. Coiffed I was not.

How was this woman going to carry her array of cosmetics, jewelry, wardrobe, and all of that camping gear? On her back? I mean, she had her own arthritic issues, especially in her neck. Naw. Never happen. She was just dreaming. I didn't have to worry about wimping out because she would never actually hike for hundreds of miles carrying her beauty essentials and house on her back. She was going nowhere without her hair dryer. Nope. I was home free here. I didn't have to worry about my joints, asking John to scoop out the kitty litter for an indeterminate amount of time, and visiting my mother in the *home*. I was good here. Julie would be onto something else. Or, shudder.....would she? Over the ensuing weeks her enthusiasm did not seem to be waning. Quite the opposite. She had become a woman possessed. I needed to either re-think my reasons for not going, my seemingly endless list of excuses, or maybe I needed to reconsider my initial reaction.

This Appalachian Trail idea was pretty far out. It's one thing to take a hike in the woods and maybe even camp overnight. A person who backpacks is really a pack-mule. I mean, think about it. Everything needed for reasonably comfortable survival has to fit in this huge, monster wardrobe that is strapped onto your back. One needs a house, a bed, a mattress, and stove just to start off. Granted, we call these things tent, sleeping bag, pad, and the stove is actually a very tiny cup-thingy that just heats water, but still. That is one large amount of equipment.

Those are just the basics. Then you have dishes, clothes, medicines, tools, food and water. All of that stuff gets rolled up and strapped onto yourself. You're talking about twenty-five pounds, if you really, really, really pack lightly. Naw. Never happen. We may have taken a few extended biking trips in the past, but we didn't need to pack camping gear and all of our food. We did the motel/bed & breakfast thing. We might have gotten sweaty and gritty as we pedaled during the day, but we could always stop at a store and buy what we needed. We bathed at the end of the day. We had all of the creature comforts we wanted, without having to strap them on. Naw. I couldn't see Julie doing this. Couldn't see myself, either.

I was sixty-one years old. Soon to be sixty-two. I was going to retire at the end of June. I filed my papers for social security. My athletic accomplishments were a thing of the past. I had run my marathons, completed several extended biking trips, finished triathlons. Every single day my body reminded me that I had likely overdone most of those things. My knees, hips, and back made known their displeasure at all the miles I ran on pavement. Since I began jogging way before it was fashionable, my footwear was not exactly what would be termed as supportive.

Kay Switzer entered the Boston Marathon in 1967, registering as K. Switzer, because at that time women were not allowed to participate. Race official, Jack Semple, tried to drag her off the course, but her boyfriend, who was running with her, shoved him aside. Hey, running a marathon takes enough energy, without having to suffer a physical assault along the way. She went on to finish with a respectable 4:20. It wasn't until 1972 that women were allowed to formally register, which was the year that Title IX was passed, providing equal opportunity for women in sports. Switzer continued her marathon career and in fact won Boston in 1974 with a time of 3:07:59 (59th overall finish). Her personal record for a marathon was 2:51:37 in Boston, 1975.

I began running in 1972. I talked Julie into running a marathon in 1982. Although we never posted times like Kay Switzer, we ran three marathons. I completed two, Julie did all three. Our best time was 3:52:34, which was not bad for running in cheap shoes, not knowing how to train, eating poorly, and being dehydrated during most of our runs. I had those accomplishments in *my* war chest. My joints ached, some were visibly swollen from osteoarthritis, and my latest back x-ray was not pretty. I was slowing down physically. I was getting older. I was getting old. No. I wasn't going to hike on the Appalachian Trail with a full pack strapped to my bony frame.

I'd sailed on by my prime. I was looking at a life of lunching with the ladies, doing crafts, playing my bagpipes, and continuing with my faithful, but mundane daily workouts at the local YMCA where I rarely broke into a sweat. I had given up skiing, biked only on level terrain, and fretted about my sun damaged skin. I was a hot mess with regard to the aging process, because I wasn't dealing with it very well. Not only did I believe I looked old, thanks to all

those years of life guarding and sunbathing, but I felt old. I had
turned sixty. That was significant. Maybe sixty was the new forty,
but I guess I missed that memo. When I looked into a mirror I saw
the skin of a spotted lizard. I saw my bony Aunt Eleanor. No. I
couldn't hike. I was just too damn old.

But then, a little teeny, weeny, tiny voice inside me said, "No,
no, no.....you aren't really *that* old."

I'm not sure at exactly what point I began to reconsider, but I
did. It was a very gradual process. I guess once I actually took on
the old role, I hit a nerve. There was that very subtle knee jerk
reaction to pull back, but then to put the knee out again. Maybe it
was Julie's continued enthusiasm as she talked about her upcoming
hike, ordering her pack and supplies, calling and telling me about
the latest Amazon hiking gizmo to arrive. Maybe it was her very
apparent silence when I rambled on and on and on about why I
couldn't join her. What had I become? Instead of feeling grateful
for the decent health that I always enjoyed, I lamented on all signs
of aging. Slowly, I seemed to be surrendering to the aging fairy. I
was staring straight into her magic wand without even trying to
fight off her spell. Where had "I" gone?

I have always, always, always been an independent girl. Tell
me I can't do something, and watch it happen. I will prove you
wrong and prove to myself that I am special. I have that inner
drive, that never-give-up spirit. I scraped, primed, and painted my
entire house by myself in my thirties, learned to play the bagpipes
and banjo in my fifties. I was the poster girl for "git er done."
That was my mantra WAY before it became trendy. Were there
any traces left of the spunk that had always fueled me? Did I have
any spirit left in these old bones and body parts? Just....maybe...I
did.

Chapter 2: Getting Ready

I began to push myself more at the YMCA. I raised my pulse well up over one hundred beats per minute and formed beads of perspiration on my forehead. I started to incorporate long walks into my weekly routine. Two miles, three miles, sometimes even four. I looked straight into the mirror at all my laugh lines, wrinkkles, freckles, and furrows.

"Girl," I said. "You are the youngest you are ever going to be. It's now or never. Get your ass out there and move! Screw the wrinkles and lizard skin. Your shit works. Use it. Now!"

It was like starting the Rocky theme song in my head. I had this. I could do this. I was joining my adventure-bestie on the Appalachian Trail, if only for one day!

At the end of my moment of inspiration, I suddenly felt better. I really did. Hey, if Jack LaLane could haul a boat with his teeth at the age of eighty, if George H.W. Bush could jump out of a plane in his ninth decade, if my husband could sail across the Atlantic at sixty-five, I sure as hell could strap on a pack and trudge a few miles through the woods. I was in. I had this.

"Jule, you know, I've been thinking.....my back has felt pretty good lately. Maybe I could meet up with you and hike for a day or two. You know. Just to show support. I could see how I feel. I'd love to say I hiked ten miles on the Appalachian Trail."

"Sandy, I'm so glad to hear you say that! I didn't recognize the whiny bitch I've been listening to! I couldn't believe what was coming out of your mouth. I thought, who is this old lady? I don't know her. Where did Sandy go? The one who is always talking ME into shit!'"

Let the training begin! I am as old as I feel, not as old as I look! And, perhaps, I don't really look *that* old. My first thought was just to meet up with Julie on the trail to hike a very non-challenging, scenic, flat section. I'd walk for the day, if my back held up. Maybe I could even do three days. That would be great.

I could say that I spent three days hiking on the Appalachian Trail, eating, sleeping, peeing and pooing in the woods. It would be a brief, albeit awesome adventure. Julie suggested this hike to me in March, and my excuses persisted until May. I was now training in earnest.

I began to sweat like an athlete on the elliptical machine, added the stair-climber, and even started lifting weights. I added laps to my swim. I began to actually visualize myself on the trail. I told everyone who I even remotely knew that I was planning to hike on the Appalachian Trail. I talked about it a lot, even though I knew nothing about the trail itself or the conditions I would be facing. I really didn't give consideration to cold, heat, bugs, water, not bathing, sleeping on the ground, or walking in the dark. All of those would-be deterrents no longer mattered to me. Mostly, I thought about whether my back would hurt from the pack I would be lugging and how I could make it as light as possible. Sidebar: my planning and my training was worthless. Completely worthless. I so very, very much underestimated just how rigorous hiking with a full pack is for anyone, regardless of their physical conditioning.

I did some research, educating myself about the Appalachian Trail, or AT, as it is referred to by those who hike it. I learned that the Appalachian Trail Conservancy was formed in 1925 to advance the proposals for making a continuous trail along the mountain crests of the eastern wilderness. Benton MacKaye, who was a forester for the US Forest Service and a planner for the Tennessee Valley Authority, pushed to construct a trail that would be maintained by local organizations. His vision was an escape from the stresses of modern life. I have to say that after spending even the little amount of time hiking that I did, I totally understand. In fact on my second day home, while standing at the kitchen sink preparing dinner and discussing all of the things I would need to do over the next couple of days said, "Fuck this shit! Send me back to the woods!" I really meant it.

The Potomac Appalachian Trail Club (PATC) was founded in 1927 to construct and supervise segments of the AT in the mid-Atlantic region. The PATC supported the establishment of Shenandoah National Park, but the design and construction of the Skyline Drive from 1931-1939 caused conflict with the ATC. This roadway was built along the crest of the Blue Ridge in the same location as the original AT. Most of it had to be relocated lower down the mountain slopes. Benton MacKaye and the PATC president Myron Avery parted ways on bad terms. Avery believed that the trail and the road could co-exist, but MacKaye would not compromise and left the ATC to become a founding member of The Wilderness Society. The Civilian Conservation Corps built the new trail and assorted structures between 1933 and 1942. The PATC then partnered with the National Park Service, in order to maintain the route.

It is a marked hiking trail extending from Springer Mountain, Georgia to Mount Katahdin, Maine. It passes through Georgia, North Carolina, Tennessee, Virginia, West Virginia, Maryland, Pennsylvania, New Jersey, New York, Connecticut, Massachusetts, Vermont, New Hampshire, and Maine. It was completed in 1937 and is now maintained by multiple trail clubs and partnerships. An extension known as the International Appalachian Trail continues northeast, crossing into Canada and on to Newfoundland, with sections going on to Greenland, Europe, and Morocco.

So. I knew nothing about this history when I first decided to hike. I knew nothing about hiking. I thought a hike was a walk on a very well-marked path through the woods. Ha. Silly me. I didn't realize it would be weaving up mountains, across ridges and fields, through towns, across rivers and streams. I did comprehend that strapping your "house to your back," would present a certain amount of strain on the body. I had no idea just how tough carrying twenty-plus pounds of gear up a mountain would be when I only weighed one hundred twenty-five pounds myself.

But then, I had done tough things in my life before. So had Julie. A person doesn't reach the age of sixty without having lived through some adversity. That old saying of "what doesn't kill you just makes you stronger," although maybe a bit on the corny sounding side, could not ring more true. Scar tissue is pretty strong. And good God, we had ourselves some wicked scar tissue. Going through an ugly divorce with children involved will grow a good crop of it. Going through two divorces will really produce a field. It was actually during Julie's second divorce that this Appalachian Trail idea was hatched.

She later told me she felt the need to get away from as many distractions as possible and have a seemingly unlimited amount of time to think. Although I have felt that way during some rough times in my own life, I can honestly say that hitting a trail in the woods would not have been my first go-to solution. I hate to admit it, but my coping strategies tended to involve microwave popcorn, Fuzzy Navel cocktails, and watching I Love Lucy reruns. I nibbled away on too much crappy food, drank more than my share of alcohol, and could probably recite the Lucy scripts without missing a line. My only consolation is telling myself I could have done worse. At least I was only a sobbing, whining, pathetic wreck for a limited amount of time. I did emerge from the ordeal. Eventually.

Chapter 3: Divorce

Divorce does some bad shit. Don't ever let someone tell you that it doesn't. Sure, if you don't let yourself become embittered, if you seize the experience to get stronger, if you keep your head up, stay positive, and not let spite and hatred become your mantras, you will likely come through it a better person. Granted, you will have some scar tissue, but that's OK. Ever notice how impervious that stuff can be?

Don't get me wrong. It certainly is possible to get divorced and emerge a total physical and emotional wreck. I've seen it happen. I have seen people who stay wrecked. I'm not judging here. Survival isn't always easy or even possible. A person may look as though thcy have done alright for themselves, but in essence, they are only very good at acting. If there was an academy award for "successful survivor of divorce" they might easily be a recipient.

It can also be the impetus needed to do things you would never have previously considered. If a person remains open to new adventures and experiences, it really can be the beginning of a new life. Divorce doesn't have to be seen as a failure. There are a couple of more positive scenarios that come to mind. We could look at the whole disconnect as a rebooting.

These days I see it as the beginning of a train trip of indefinite destination. We board the train as a couple, excited and hopeful about our trip. Along the way, we start to detrain at various points of interest. Sometimes we can't wait to get back on the track, and other times it's with great reluctance that we return to our seats. Finally, after many days, months and years of sometimes ambivalent travel, we just don't return to the same train. This departure can be wretchedly painful or just genuine relief. The feelings are impossible to predict.

I used to think of my early divorce time as riding a roller coaster. I knew there was going to be some uphills, some drop offs, some crazy turns, and some upside down loops. I would unlatch my safety bar, climb out of the coaster car, have some excitement, and just get on with visiting other rides in the park.

Over the years I have talked with hundreds of divorced folks. Most were women, perhaps because they are often more open about sharing their feelings and personal experiences. In most cases, all were struggling in some fashion. Maybe it was to figure out what went wrong, why their connection fizzled over time, why they felt the need to leave or were left. I heard of no simple answers in all of my conversations.

Julie tells me she thought that after her first marriage imploded for a variety of reasons, that she was being given a second chance. She, like myself, had married very young. As we mature, we hopefully stop blaming our former partners and start reflecting and examining our own behaviors.

When her second marriage crumbled she said, "I thought I'd really found my soul mate. This was going to be the forever one, the guy I'd go to the grave with. But when I realized he wasn't the person I thought he was, I knew I had to end it. I felt like I'd lost my soul, because I just didn't know myself anymore. I couldn't trust my judgment."

These days, I have to dig pretty deep into the moldy mind corners to dredge up my divorce archives. They have been bundled and stored for decades, going back to 1987 and the era of big hair, disco, dirty dancing, and bad clothing styles. But, when I hear a song, see a sappy movie from that time, run into an acquaintance from way back then, the memories flood back. Some of that water is murky and putrid, some as pure as a mountain stream.

I am not the same person I was in 1987. Of course, anyone who sees me now will certainly agree that "ain't no lie." My hair is no longer big and brown, my face looks like a road map, and my body, well that is still pretty okay. I often say that I look pretty good from the neck down at about forty yards out. Aside from the physical changes, I am not the same complacent, semi-dependent, man-pleasing, terrified-of-being-alone-girl that I once was. I mean, hey, I kept my own name before it was fashionable! There was an independent bitch in there waiting to get out. She just needed a clear path. Or at least a path with a minimum of prickly brier bushes crowding it. Divorce paved that way for me. Wonder Woman I am not, but tenacious like my grandmas, sensible like my dad, kind like my mom, and one shitload wiser than I once was; I can own.

Everyone who steps into the tunnel of marriage takes the risk of emerging through the divorce exit. I recently found (okay, I did go looking) the book I claimed to be writing during the first few years of my divorce. Turns out, it really is nothing more than a poorly written journal with foul language. I didn't realize my writing skills were that bad and that my repertoire for filth was that broad. Clearly, they were, and it was.

I did, however, come across a few excerpts that I found acceptable to reprint. "And then you are finally divorced. The day I got my final papers in the mail, I cried. I'm not really sure why, as I certainly didn't want to be married to the man who left me for his younger, long haired secretary. Perhaps it was my feeling of vulnerability. Clearly, he was making a different partner choice, and that was causing a profound emptiness that seemed to completely swallow me. I suppose it was the finality of it all. For those next few days, I kept waiting to feel something different, something profound. I didn't know how I should expect to feel, but it seemed that there should be some sort of revelation. I thought that when I saw the divorce papers with all of their legal terms I would feel purged. I only felt empty, sad, and like a failure. But, I also felt just a wee spark of hope. I felt like if I just gave myself a chance to be OK, I really would be. And so would Jamie, my eight year old daughter."

Looking back, I was very, very much OK. I began to thrive. The first self-improvement project I took on was that of getting myself pretty teeth. Yup. My overbite was going to be history. I made myself an appointment with the orthodontist and followed through with his first suggestion of getting four teeth pulled. However, I insisted, against my dentist's advice, to have all four teeth pulled at once. "We don't like to do that," he told me.

"I know. Please do it anyway. I will be fine. Just numb me up with a lot of Novocain," I answered with way more bravado than I was actually feeling.

Soon I would be sprouting a smile with four gaping holes in my mouth. After the holes where my teeth once lived healed over, I was fitted with a full set of braces. Yes, they hurt. A lot. I came to understand, very quickly, why getting four teeth pulled simultaneously with only a local anesthetic was maybe not the best idea. The pain from the newly vacated teeth was bad enough, but when the orthodontist wired my mouth up with a full set of braces, upper and lower, I could not chew for two weeks and dreamed every night that all of my teeth were falling out.

Braces in place and a few months of single-woman-single-parent status on board, I decided that a vacation was in order. In fact, it was way, way, way overdue. I deserved this. I packed up my newly acquired independence, my little Nissan Sentra car with no AC and drove to Disney World over winter break with my daughter. I left at two in the morning, and I cannot put into words the thrill I felt as I drove across the first state border. I knew then that my daughter and I would be fine. I suppose I should add that it was only about twenty-five miles to Pennsylvania, but still, it was a benchmark. I was heading south with no man.

On a sidebar, that entire vacation cost three hundred dollars. And that included the two three-day passes I bought from a scalper at the front gate. Okay. So I live on the frugal side. I prefer that term to cheap. Mostly, it was just that I pretty much had very little money and a limited amount of child support. I learned to really, really stretch a dollar. Actually, explaining the budget of my first year as a single girl would take up at least a full chapter.

Did we have a great time at Disneyland? Well, I suppose that would be stretching the truth. It was a growthful thing to do. It was a step forward in my new life of independence, and I am glad for the experience. However, my now thirty-seven year old daughter remembers very little of the trip, likely because she has repressed her feelings. Too bad I could not have repressed more of my own.

It is about a twenty-four hour drive to Orlando from our home in Corning, NY. Since it would be just me driving, I divided the trip into two days down and two days back. Our half-way point was Asheville, North Carolina, to stay with one of my college roommates. Because of my bleak financial situation, motels were out of the question. Besides, it would be good to see Carol again; too many years had passed for us. Sadly, today the thing I remember most about our short stay with Carol is when my daughter told her very excitedly that "Daddy's new girlfriend has long hair and a beautiful figure just like Barbie."

"How nice," Carol replied.

Why do I remember shit like this? Our digs in Florida would be with my brother's in-laws. They were very kind to us, and we stayed for three days with them. But since our time was primarily spent at Disney World, we actually just ate and slept in their double-wide parked in the retirement community. Jamie threw-up after dinner the first night. My funds were so very limited that the only food we ate in the Disney Park were packs of peanut butter and cheese crackers. They cost twenty-five cents each at the time. And we drank water. No wonder she threw-up. Plus, we got drenched in a torrential rainstorm and had to strip naked in the parking lot. Yes, I was discreet. At least, I believe that I was. The only dry items I had in my car were a couple of jackets and two afghans. I suppose it is with good reason that Jamie has repressed this vacation memory. Admittedly, it is a bit foggy for me.

My first do-it-yourself project was to paint my entire house, inside and out, by myself. One reason I did this was to change as many things as I could, hoping to erase, to the best of my ability, evidence of the man I once lived with. The other reason was that it was badly needed. The outside was peeling and beginning to show all the signs of neglect. I wanted my house to convey a totally-got-her-shit-together kinda girl. I mowed my lawn, cleaned my chimney, planted my garden, trimmed my bushes. I suffered a minor setback there when I cut the electrical cord to the trimmer in half, sliced my finger, and had to halt the project. I resumed my quest after getting stitched up in the ER. I worked full time, volunteered at my daughter's school, and continued with my daily jogging routine. The latter activity was not only for my physical and mental health, but also helped me to keep up my appearance just in case I ever wanted to attract another man. That wasn't presently on my radar screen. Maybe someday. Who knew?

I survived divorce. Eventually, I even thrived. So, when Julie began the process of her second divorce I understood why she told me she needed to figure out why she made the decisions leading her into the land of marriage failure.

"Clearly I have poor judgment when it comes to choosing men. My man-picker seems to be broken. Or maybe I never got one," she said to me and my husband shortly after the departure of husband number two.

"In fact, that's going to be my answer if I ever get asked out on another date. And, it's what I'm pretty sure got me my school nurse job. At the end of the interview, they asked me about any areas of weakness I might have. I thought about it, looked around at all of the women in the room, and then just blurted it out. I also mentioned that my parents had owned a bakery, and I had the secret lemon cookie recipe. They cracked up."

One of them said, "You're hired!" Julie added.

My husband was aghast.

"Oh my God, you can't say that! Do you have any idea what kind of a challenge that is for a man?"

"Oh. Bad answer?" asked Julie.

"Bad answer," said my husband.

"It wasn't bad for getting my job," said Julie.

"No. Maybe not. But it won't be good for dating. Besides, maybe it was the secret recipe that got you the job," said John.

"OK. I'll think about it," answered Julie. "Hey, have you ever eaten any of the lemon cookies?"

Chapter 4: Planning the Adventure

Having finally given up the excuse routine, I decided I would make the effort to carry what would be a very heavy pack for me. Anything over fifteen pounds seemed very heavy because as I said, I only weigh about one hundred twenty-five pounds to begin with. I would hike a section, albeit a very tiny one, of the Appalachian Trail with my bestie in adventures, newly-almost-divorced Julie. We would add this, not to our "bucket" lists, but to our "done it" lists.

Every day I would get a call from her telling me of some new hiking gizmo she purchased from Amazon. Don't get me wrong here. I love Amazon. What's not to love? A credit card and Amazon Prime are a must-have for any girl. Still. This hiking thing really seemed to be taking over her life. And it was threatening mine.

"I got my pack! I love it! Wait til you see!"

"My brother, Bruce, ordered me a head lamp! I can't wait to see it!"

"My cute little stove came! OMG! It's so tiny!"

"I got my tent. It's a two-person, so you don't need to worry about ordering one."

"My sleeping bag and pad came."

"Wait til you see this water purification system!"

"Sandy, you really should get your pack if you want to do this," Julie reminded me during one of her calls.

Yes. I guess I did. I was in. All the way. I needed to quit stalling. Unless I wanted to try and cram everything into my non-hiking-kid-sized backpack, I needed to begin stocking my very empty hiking locker.

I thought of just ordering online like Julie did, but since my knowledge of gear was so meager, well, non-existent, I decided I better check out what was available in an actual store. Had I not had the conversation with Gary at the YMCA, who was sweating on the elliptical machine next to me, I never would have known about the Eastern Mountain Sports store located in Ithaca, which was about forty-five minutes away. I would likely have gone to Sears. Maybe even Walmart. What did I know? Julie had done her homework prepping for this hike. I had not. And I hated to keep asking her what I should do, because it made me feel even more unprepared than I already was. Still. I needed to take a definitive step here. I needed to actually look at some gear.

Eastern Mountain Sports, (EMS) is a chain of stores that cater to the serious, outdoor, rugged, really-mean-business-kick-ass-hiker type people. At this point in my sixty-one year old life, I very clearly was not one of those people. I wouldn't exactly call myself a wimp, I mean I could rock that elliptical machine at the YMCA, as long as there was no resistance or incline. And my crawl stroke was to be admired. But, mountain goat, I was not. So. Okay. Maybe I was a little wimpy. Maybe I would never be a kick-ass hiker type. But then, I wouldn't know unless I tried it. I was definitely going to try this. Really. Show me the trail. This baby was mine.

Off to the Ithaca EMS! I mapquested, plugged in my GPS for backup, and backed on out of the school parking lot. Have I mentioned I am now retired? At the time of the hiking preparation, I was not. I was still working as a school counselor. I liked my job alright, but I would certainly like not having to work a great deal more. My first trip to EMS was scheduled for after work, squashed in between all of the other duties like visiting my mom at her assisted living place, grocery shopping, mowing the lawn, house cleaning....you get the picture. My job was getting in the way of my leisure time. It was with much enthusiasm that I was counting down the days. My job was interfering with my hiking prep.

The hike was going to be my kick off adventure after I closed the chapter on my professional life. Actually, I liked to think of it as slamming the book closed. I was done. I had liked working in the schools, but I was just so very ready to like something else. I digress. Back to trail prep.

I already had my hiking shoes, which I purchased at Famous Brands in Watkins Glen. They were pretty blue-violet Merrill Capra Bolt lightweights. I don't know why a company would invest in making their hiking shoes pretty, because very quickly they are going to be brown. Or black. They will be totally filthy. Of all the camping gear I bought, this is the only brand name I can tell you, because shoes have their label printed on them. I suppose it is for advertising purposes.

Shoes are extremely visible. Who sees the pad resting under the sleeping bag? Or, for that matter, the sleeping bag? The company would have to print huge, block letters on them. That would make them ugly. No wonder there are just tiny little tags attached. If I were a more serious, dedicated, thoughtful, and informed hiker, I would be making a detailed list, describing each item, and why it is needed in the backpack. I would tell the cost, the weight, and the brand. I will not be doing that. This isn't a hiking manual. If that is what you are looking for, you are perusing the wrong reading material. This is closer to a "what not to do when hiking" guide.

Finding my way to the EMS store with no difficulty and marching into the store, full of confidence, possessing a bit of attitude, I wasted no time announcing that I was going to be hiking a section of the Appalachian Trail, and I needed gear. I needed everything. I didn't even have a water bottle. Also, I readily admitted that I knew absolutely nothing about hiking. Maybe that was foolish because I could see the dollar signs reflecting in the eyes of the salesman who figured he had struck pay dirt with this novice. He would sell her the best of everything, which of course, would correspond directly with the most expensive. Ha! Little did he know how frugal, okay, cheap, I was. While he was likely calculating his commission, my eyes settled on the SALE sign. Years and years of little or no money had trained my bargain sensors.

They were finely tuned. I could always sniff out a sale. Any time, any store, anywhere, if there was a SALE sign in there, I would find it. Fast. Time warp speed.

The salesman, sensing that he had fresh prey, ready to unload the better part of her paycheck, herded me directly to the wall of backpacks, because that was what I asked to see first. Of course, he pulled down the most expensive pack, and granted, it was very nice. He showed me how to measure my torso for the proper fitting and adjusted the straps. Yes. It was comfortable. And $200 more than I wanted to spend.

"What about that one," I asked, pointing to a smaller, much less expensive pack.

"Oh, you wouldn't want that. It's youth sized. It wouldn't fit you properly," he assured me.

"Oh. Okay. But could I just try it? I mean, I'm not that big," I pushed.

"Certainly," he said, as politely as he could now that he could already feel his very substantial sale suddenly turning teeny weeny.

Fortunately for him, unfortunate for me, he was right. It was just a little too small. I could have used it if I had to make do, but it wasn't very comfortable. I looked back at the wall of packs, and my eyes lasered in on yet another SALE number.

"How about this one? Is this a pretty okay kind of pack?" I asked.

"Well, it isn't the same quality as the first one you tried on, but this is a pretty good item. The only problem you might have is you may find it a little small. This is only forty-five liters, and if you're out on the trail for more than a day, you really need a sixty liter pack," the guy explained.

"Oh, that shouldn't be a problem. I'm going with my girl-friend, and she's carrying the tent, stove, and water purification things. I'm only going to be out a few days so I don't need much," I started to ramble.

Realizing that the guy now likely thought I was a lesbian,

because I mentioned my girlfriend, I quickly inserted something about my husband into the conversation. I'm not really sure why I felt a need to do this because I am totally very cool with lesbian, gay, transgender, transsexual. Whatever. I don't care. As long as you are a nice person, I am not interested in what you do in the bedroom and what equipment might be needed. C'est la vie. Besides, this was Ithaca, not Woodchuck Hollow. Everyone knows everything is okay in Ithaca.

Some years ago when I was on one of the bike trips with Julie, I recall standing at the front desk of a motel in Kingston, Canada. Checking in for the night, paying our bill, and getting our room key, we turned toward the elevator.

I still do not know what possessed me to announce, "We aren't lesbians. We're just good friends. I'm not sure why I'm telling you this, but just thought maybe you should know."

Yes. I actually said that. And yes, the woman behind the desk just stared at us, speechless. She didn't even smile. She just stared with her mouth open. I don't know why I remember this moment so vividly, but I do.

I also remember Julie saying, "Jesus Christ, WTF were you thinking? You do know she's certain now we're lesbians. I can't believe you just said that."

I don't know why I said it either. It was like the filter between my brain and my mouth suddenly short-circuited. I know I have repressed other events in my life. I wish I could add this one to that pile.

Back to EMS in Ithaca. "Can I see some sleeping bags? I want a really lightweight one. Doesn't have to be one of those subzero kind because I'm only hiking in the summer. What's the best kind at the lower end of your price range?" I asked, unabashedly.

I totally admit that when it comes to shopping, sales, and the prospect of saving money I have absolutely no shame. None.

"All our bags are of excellent quality, but the ones on this end are a bit less expensive," explained the sales guy.

By now, I'm sure he realized I was not only clueless about hiking, but I was cheap. And of course, a lesbian. A cheap lesbian. He pulled down the sleeping bag and encouraged me to put one of the pads underneath it, and then lay down to see how it would feel. That made sense, although I have to say it was a little embarrassing to be laying on the floor of the EMS store. I don't know why I should have been embarrassed at this because not much seems to bother me anymore. I have become shameless as I've aged, and although I don't think this is an especially bad way to be, I suppose there are times when perhaps I should show more self respect, more pride. There is still a streak inside of me that wants to be separated from those who lurk in the Walmart parking lot wearing tube tops and pajamas.

The self-inflating mattress pad seemed comfy enough under the poofy sleeping bag. Not a mattress by any means, but certainly better than laying on the hard ground. I especially liked the self-inflating aspect, because I could not picture myself puffing and huffing at the end of a day of hiking to blow up my cushion. I certainly wasn't about to add the weight of an air pump. I was extremely aware of how much things weighed and kept doing the math. My pack was growing heavier by the minute, and I hadn't even purchased the thing yet.

I settled on the forty-five liter pack and a two pound and four ounce sleeping bag with a handy little storage bag to stuff it in. Incidentally, the two pounds and four ounces included that little bag. I picked out an orange pad and also bought a head lamp. There. I had four items. My journey was almost beginning.

Driving home, I imagined myself walking along a beautiful trail, pack strapped on, the wind blowing my hair, Julie and I discussing days gone by as well as what lay ahead for us. I did not see rocks on my imaginary walk. Nor, did I see dried up streams, spider-bites, mountains, rain, and ninety-plus degree temperatures. And I didn't see myself getting sick from heat and dehydration.

"Jule," I called on my way home from the hiking store, carrying my new backpacking items in the butt end of Lucy. My car's name is Lucy. Named for Lucille Ball, or the fictional Lucy Ricardo, from the I Love Lucy TV series, which I love. And my husband hates. Maybe because he has tired of the reruns that I can watch hundreds, seriously, I mean hundreds of times and not get tired of them.

I know the scripts. I know them very well. I could ace a test on them, be it essay or multiple choice. It's my comfort food of television and so I love Maroon colored Lucy, which is close enough to red for me to have named her Lucy. My car is a girl. I don't think I have ever had a boy car. I'm not sure why. I just think of myself in girl cars.

"I got gear! I bought a backpack, sleeping bag, pad, and head light. You have to check out this store. I want to come back and look at the clothes. I'm thinking I'll just get my hiking pants here. Maybe a hat, too. The one I use for sailing isn't that comfortable," I very, very, very excitedly explained to Julie.

"Wow! You went all out! Where's the store again? I definitely need to go. I still want to pick up a few more things. Amazon is good, but I want to try on the clothes first. I need pants, shorts, and one of those lightweight shirts. Maybe I'll get a hat, too. I was going to wear my cowboy hat, but I'll check out what they have. The cowboy hat's kind of bulky."

One week later, following the outdoor luncheon our friend, Janice, had thrown, where we impressed the shit out of all the other women there as we talked about our upcoming hike, the two of us walked into the Eastern Mountain Sports store in Ithaca. The same salesman greeted us, so I introduced Julie as my friend, not my girlfriend. Hmm. Maybe that left him wondering about where my actual girlfriend was.

This was an uneventful, yet fairly productive shopping spree, and we left the store with the kind of hiking pants that had the little straps and buttons at the side allowing them to double as capris.

They are made of that very lightweight, breathable material that allows for quick drying. Had I not quickly snipped the label off, I could tell you just exactly what they are made out of and also reference a brand.

Julie bought a pair of shorts made out of the same material. I no longer wear shorts because I am too self conscious and vain about the sun damage on my legs. The skin looks like a cross between crepe paper and lizard scales. Yes. It's ugly. I know I am being ridiculous because who really looks at the legs of a sixty plus year old woman? And, I should just be grateful that my legs work. Well, I am thankful for that, but I still lament the years I spent baking in the sun and aging my skin. I am way more prune than I am plum these days.

I wear capris pants in the summer which are certainly cooler than long pants, and they successfully hide a lot of the sun carnage. Sometimes I wear those tight biking type shorts, with a long t-shirt to cover my butt. I find those suck in saggy skin really well. But mostly, it is capris pants in the summer. They are very forgiving.

As mentioned earlier, I look pretty good from a distance of about forty yards out. With clothing, of course. Actually, I am thinking that once retired, maybe I could be successful in the modeling profession. You know, where they have those before and after pictures? The before person looks like they have been photographed immediately after getting out of bed with the puffy eyes, bloated face and hair sticking straight up in the back? The fact that I also have all of those age spots from the sun just adds to the horror. I could be that person. If I were paid enough, I would do it. No problem. Really. I look like that anyway. I may as well cash in on it.

We also each bought long sleeved shirts made out of material that wicks the moisture and dries quickly. And they had a small strap and button so that the sleeves would be held in place when rolled up. We browsed around the store looking for other hiking items we may not have thought of and that we would be able to improvise out of things we already had, so we wouldn't have to actually spend more money. Yes. Julie had a frugal streak as well. It just wasn't as pronounced as mine.

Looking around, we found a light weight metal hiking dish cost twenty dollars. Seriously. It was a cereal bowl for God's sake. And a spoon was almost as pricey. Really? Silverware, especially the cheap stuff, was not that heavy. We would pass on those items. I'd go to The Dollar Store when I got home.

We did look at some of the freeze dried food that EMS carried. I studied the ingredients, as I always do when shopping for food and found them to be loaded with sodium. I knew nothing about freeze-dried foods, but I did know if I ingested that much sodium I would bloat like a puffball mushroom. It would be a good idea to check for other brands.

Leaving EMS with our new backpacking items, we were cranked. We were well on our way to fully stocked packs. Appalachian Trail, watch out. These bitches were serious! Over the next couple of weeks, we continued to gather items. Julie returned to Amazon land. We discovered a small hiking store right in our own hometown, Ranger Outfitters. This place is amazing, and we can't thank Chris enough for his patience in answering our questions and making suggestions. From here we bought organic non-chemical deer and tick repellent, long sleeved fleece shirts, water bottles, and an assortment of freeze dried meals. There was still more sodium in these than I wanted, but apparently all of that stuff is pretty loaded with it. At least there were a few vegetarian entrees.

Although I very occasionally eat meat, it is certainly not often. I don't believe I've ingested pork since 1993. At least not intentionally. I do eat sea creatures. My reasoning for this is that they eat each other anyway. Little fish eat bigger fish, bigger fish eat even bigger fish. So, I am actually a top to bottom feeder with regard to seafood, because I eat catfish as well as tuna. Still, it does bother me to eat the fish, especially when I think about them flopping around as they slowly suffocate.

During the summer, I feed little pieces of bread to the fish that swim under the dock where our sailboat is parked. As the summer goes on, the fish actually become conditioned to seeing me on the dock and associate me with the bread that drops into their water kitchen. They swarm like piranhas whenever I step off the boat. I get pissed when I see people fishing because I consider these little guys to be my fish. I don't like the thought of someone filleting them. They are my pets.

And, I just can't bring myself to eat a lobster because I know they are put into boiling water while still alive. That really, really tears at my heart. I don't know for sure if they can feel the pain, but whatever the case, swimming in boiling water cannot be a pleasant experience, and it does kill them. No lobster for me.

Occasionally, and I do mean very, very occasionally, I will eat a free range chicken. I don't like the idea of it, but when I am not feeling well, chicken soup always comes to mind, and it does taste so good. I think it makes me feel better. But I can't stand the thought of the factory farms and all of the suffering that goes on in them. That is why I don't eat meat. Plus, I love pigs and think that cows are adorable. I couldn't eat my cat or dog. How can I eat these other furry creatures? My hiking partner, Julie, does not exactly share my philosophy. I mean, she's not a factory farm kind of girl, but she hunts. And every year, I tell her that I have put a hex upon her hunting skills and am sending out survival vibes to Bambi's family. Some years it works, some years it doesn't. At least she never offers venison to me.

For the sake of our hike, our friendship, and because the hike was her idea, and she is carrying more of the gear, I did agree to eat a freeze dried chicken dinner, if necessary. And I wouldn't complain. Hopefully, I would not get diarrhea. No one can say I don't try to play with the team. I am very cooperative and willing to compromise. Just don't ask me to eat steak. Or bacon, lamb, duck, goose, pheasant, turkey, and whatever else flies or walks that could be considered as food in the western world.

We have some friends who traveled to Africa to visit their daughter in the Peace Corps. The people living in the village were very excited to serve a special dinner to Dr. Michelle's parents and cooked up a feast featuring the local delicacy. It. Was. Roasted. Pussycat. Yes. Served with the head and paws still attached, just like what we see at a pig roast. They were appalled, grossed out, totally disgusted and emotionally devastated because they had a kitty back home. Deciding it would be best not to create an international incident, they ate kitty. What choice did they have? But for the remainder of the three weeks they were in the south of Africa they subsisted mostly on bagel type rolls, wine and beer. Dr. Michelle's father lost fifteen pounds. Thankfully, we are not faced with eating our house pets here in the states. Eating farm animals is painful enough.

Over the next few weeks, we continued adding items to our packs. As is sometimes the case when leaving home for an extended period of time, we over packed. Knowing we would be out on the trail in the middle of the woods, away from all amenities, with no stores to re-stock, we went a little overboard. Think about it. We needed to carry everything we would and could possibly need on our backs or stuffed into our pockets or belly pouches. Think about the things you use every day and just take for granted because you get to put them back on the shelf or in the closet. You don't have to actually carry bottles, lotions, appliances, your bed, mattress, kitchen, etc. with you, on your person.

At the time of departure, my pack contained the following: sleeping bag, pad, pillow, head lamp, two extra AA batteries, small hand towel, rain jacket and pants, pair of socks, pair of underpants, fleece shirt, pair of tights to be used as pajama bottoms (they are actually what I wear under my kilt when playing bagpipes with the Crystal City Pipe and Drum Corps), bandanna, safari type hat with brim, one pair flip flops, pair of hiking poles, pair of extra tips for hiking poles, hair brush, reading glasses, small notebook, pen, cereal bowl (which is actually a dog food dish purchased at The

Dollar Store), spoon, nail clippers, small scissors, small forceps (remember, we are nurses), Band-Aids, medications (antibiotics, anti-inflammatories, muscle relaxants, anti-diarrhea pills, laxatives, vitamins, Lisinopril for my BP, eye drops for my iritis), sunscreen, chapstick, Purell, two water bottles, large garbage bag, food (eight protein bars, bag of high protein cereal, trail mix, three freeze dried meals, ten teabags, five packages of hot chocolate, one small package of powdered milk, ten packs of powdered fruit juice, bag of almonds, two pouches of tuna fish), belly bag (to carry food, etc. around my waist), two water bottle holders, small bottle of vodka, small bottle peach schnapps, small bottle of whiskey.

These little bottles of cheer were the very tiny one shot size. They would not add much weight to my pack, but they sure could add some relaxation at the end of our day. The food I packed was supposed to be enough for three days. Yeah. I packed too much stuff. Looking back, I should have left the extra batteries and packed toilet paper.

Chapter 5: Telling Friends and Family

Deciding I really wanted to hike on the Appalachian Trail was monumental for me. I transitioned almost instantly from a whiny, excuse making, gray haired, wrinkly bitch to a totally enthusiastic gray haired, still wrinkly-but-more-invested-in-skin-creams girl. Yeah. I was hardly ever a bitch anymore. It's hard to be perfect.

Once I decided I was going to do this, I jumped off the hiking cliff in talking about it. Where I was once obsessed with the reasons why I could not hike, I now became obsessed with the hike and how I was going to succeed. Even if I only lasted just three days, I would be able to say that I hiked a section of the Appalachian Trail, and I slept in the woods. Almost by myself. It would just be us two girls. Julie and me. Sixty plus year old women hanging out like pioneers. Except that we would also have our cell phones. And freeze dried food. Maybe a wee bit of vodka, whiskey, and schnapps, too.

I started talking about my impending hike to everyone I came into contact with. And I do mean everyone. Yes. Everyone. Since my retirement would be happening just a few weeks before this big hike, I also shared that news as well. Certainly the cashier at Wegmans is interested. And the teller at the Credit Union. Let's not forget the woman tallying up the bill for my oil change and tire rotation. Oh yes. I spared no one.

"Well, I won't be working much longer. I retire this year. Yeah. I'm really looking forward to it," I would begin my monologue.

It was generally a monologue, because exactly what is my captured, uninterested audience going to say?

"I am so excited about retiring. I worked as a nurse for ten years, and I've been in education for twenty-six. I bought a year back which gives my twenty-seven. Did you know you could do that? If you're part of the New York State Retirement system, any work you did for the state counts toward retirement. Like me. I worked as a lifeguard in Hornell for seven summers. Then, I worked in the dining hall when I was a student at Oswego. I substituted for a couple of years when I first graduated, and that all added up to a year toward my retirement. I mean, it costs some money to buy the time back, and it keeps going up. You know how nothing's free. But still, it's worth it. Because once you buy it back it counts as your work time, and then it's added to your retirement. Did you know that military time counts? I'm really glad I bought my time back when I did. You really should look into it if you ever worked for any kind of city or state thing. I mean, if you worked in a state park, even if you picked up trash, that counts," I would ramble on and on and on.

Now I suppose some of my information actually could be deemed as useful. I recently spoke with my friend, Rosemary, who seriously didn't know about the buy-back thing. She looked into it and is able to retire six months early. She is thrilled. And I do have to report, I am feeling smug that it was me who helped her achieve early dismissal from kindergarten. I don't know how recently you have visited a kindergarten class, but if you in any way regard this as an easy job, you really ought to reconsider.

Imagine being responsible for twenty-something four, five, and six year old children. Some are barely toilet trained. And those who are rarely wipe. Certainly few, if any, wash their hands after their bathroom visits. Nose picking, butt scratching, whining, crying, pushing, shoving and punching are happening all day long. Maybe that seems familiar, and you just think of your own children or your spouse. But when these little people aren't your own family, it can be very difficult to manage their behavior in a manner that will not get you fired. Or arrested. Leaving this six months before the intended date of departure is truly the gift of time. Like an early release program.

It did not take me very long to realize that none of the people I cornered and spewed retirement and hiking information to were interested, except for Rosemary, regarding the time buy back deal which got her out of kindergarten early. She did not care about the hike. Aside from a very few close friends and family, no one cared that (A) I was going to retire and (B) I was going on a hike. In my more rational moments I could understand this, putting myself in the position of the poor soul I had cornered with the details of my work life and why it was good to be retiring. Of course, I always followed that with an extremely tedious description of the contents of my new backpack which would include an especially boring ramble about the importance of not having too much weight. Oh, yes. I certainly was a delight. The thing is, until just recently, I didn't actually consider just how inappropriate, but also utterly obnoxious, my diatribe was sounding.

People have their own lives and problems and professions to deal with. The news of my retirement and backpacking trip were not only of no interest to them, I was actually being annoying. Me. Annoying. Who would have thought? This behavior is not new. Not if I reflect honestly upon my past. When I was going through my divorce I would tell absolutely everyone I encountered that my husband had left me. And that he had a girlfriend. A long-haired, divorcee. I spared no details. None. I. Told. Everyone. Everything.

No one escaped my troubled tale. Grocery clerk, librarian, guy who changed my oil, guy who rotated my tires, my daughter's teacher (I made a special trip to the school for that one. I don't recall including the principal, but that was only because I didn't happen to run into him on that day.), all relatives, all friends, all work colleagues, and sadly, even the patients I admitted to the hospital. That last one got me into trouble with my supervisor, as it certainly should have. I was clearly out of control. Panting and puffing through labor pains is no time to hear about your nurse's pathetic personal life. Fresh out of anesthesia after a hysterectomy is no better. Yes. I told these people that my husband had left. Always, always, I included additional information about the girlfriend, describing her in way more detail than anyone was interested in hearing about.

I would like to think I have not been quite as bad talking about my hike. And the impending retirement. At least they are positive events. It shows I am moving forward in life, seeking out adventures and new experiences, embarking on my quest for self actualization. Well, maybe it is more of a quest to collect my pension and take a walk in the woods with a heavy pack. At least I'm not sobbing when I annoy people with this scenario.

I suppose I felt the need to tell everyone in my path because I didn't want to be thought of as just another new retiree spending her time going out to lunch, complaining about why things aren't the way they used (should) be, and talking about an upcoming trip to Florida. I guess I still wanted to be thought of as vital, adventuresome, energetic, someone who was not only taking the road less traveled, but taking the unmarked path through the woods. I guess the reason that I rambled on incessantly to Julie with my multitude of excuses was actually due to fear. I was afraid that I wouldn't be able to carry my pack, I wouldn't be able to complete even a day on the trail. If I didn't try, I couldn't fail.

My entire life has blessed me with the ability to pretty much do whatever I want, whenever I want. Run ten miles? No problem. Bike fifty miles? Done. Climb on the roof to clean my chimney? Easy. Well, not exactly easy. But, I could do it if I looped a rope around the chimney to pull myself up the steep pitch. I am afraid of heights so this particular feat was something to be especially proud of being able to accomplish.

So, last year when the pain in my lower back literally reduced me to crawling on all fours and yelping, I was humbled. I was extremely humbled. This seventh decade of my life was certainly bulldozing its way in! Clearly, I should and could not do some of the things I did in my twenties, thirties, forties, and fifties. My joints now talked to me. Everyday. Sometimes, they hollered loudly. I couldn't punish my body like I once did.

However, still wanting to do all the things I had always done, I pushed. Aging ain't for the timid, right? We all live with some denial when it comes to things we just can't quite do like we used to, if indeed we can even do them at all. We all have some diffi-culty accepting we have slowed down. Our overdrive gear is gone. Regarding my upcoming hike, I would be checking the ground before I planted a foot, or a pole, to make sure the ground was safe.

The more people I told about my hiking plans, the more I learned about backpacking. I picked up some of the terminology. For example, prior to my decision to go for this adventure, I never heard the term, "section hiker." This is the moniker applied to those folks who aren't going to hike all the way from Springer Mountain, Georgia to Mount Katahdin, Maine in one block of time. Section hikers pick out different chunks of the trail to do over various intervals of time. Maybe a weekend, maybe a week, or if they can commit to a longer length of time, they do. It may take them years to complete the entire twenty-one hundred mile trek, but eventually they do.

Actually, it is Julie's plan to hike the entire trail. Not me. No. I am not that disciplined. I don't think I'll mind stinking for a few days because I can't bathe, but I don't want extended periods of poor hygiene. I like eating my fruits and vegetables, but because they are too heavy to carry, will be giving them up. Plus, I have my other interests. I'm like Billy Mink in the Thornton Burgess animal stories that I read as a child. I have multiple skills, albeit I'm not especially good at any of them. Except I do think I am quite good at organizing things. I suppose that comes from being bossy. I admit to being very bossy. My husband tells me I am a dilettante. I suppose that maybe I am. I just like the variety. I enjoy swimming, biking, playing my bagpipes, banjo, guitar, har-monica, piano and trumpet. Of course, I have to admit that I play none of the aforementioned instruments well, but I still enjoy trying. I also like to read, sew, cook, drink wine, and yes, write.

I would most definitely be a section hiker, and a mini one at that. My goal is fifty miles. Clearly, my confidence is growing, because my original plan was to eke out ten miles. This is a good thing. I am feeling stronger, more vital. Anything beyond fifty, for me, will be amazing. And to be fair, I can only expect my husband to tend to the four kitty litter boxes for a limited amount of time. He is nice to my cats, but he just doesn't share the same enthusiasm for them that I do. I figured ten days would be max for him to patrol the litter boxes. Even though they are able to go outside, they prefer indoor plumbing. I have watched them nap in the sun all afternoon on our deck, stand up to stretch, and prance inside to pee. They will even run to the box, like they have been holding it. I suppose I should be very grateful that John is willing to even scoop for a day, let alone nearly two weeks. Plus, they don't have very good aim, and someone keeps missing the box. That is very gross, and it stinks.

Yes. They have become high maintenance pussycats regarding their toileting habits. And then there is feeding time. They. Are. Fussy. They both want canned food but can't decide what flavor they like. What they inhale one day goes untouched the next. When that happens the dishes must be rinsed off or they won't eat out of them at all. I mean, the food can't just be emptied out. The dishes absolutely must be rinsed and all traces of the rejected food gone. Otherwise they howl. They don't just meow. They howl. The more I think about this, the more I am appreciating my hus-band. I will be sure and praise him for this. A lot. I may want to stay longer in the woods. Or, take another trip.

Back when I told my mom I was going to ride my bike across New York State with Julie and I called her from the Vermont border, telling her that I was going to keep going all the way to Gloucester, Massachusetts, she said, "Oh no, Sandra! Don't do that! Come home! You've gone far enough! Your little girl needs you!"

She was always good with the guilt thing. Yes. I was raised Catholic. FYI, my little girl had just finished her junior year in college. Not only did she not need me, she did not miss me and was pleased to have the house to herself. And her friends. I was forty-five years old at the time. Telling my father about the bike trip was really easy. He just said, "Oh."

And if he were alive today, he would probably say the same thing, accompanied by, "Why would you want to do a thing like that?"

Now, my mom was ninety-two. Telling her that I was going to be hiking would be easier. She lives at UpDyke's Willow Ridge in Hornell, New York. It's an assisted living facility, and her primary concern is her hair appointment on Wednesday morning. Me, taking a hike, really won't impact her as long as my husband takes Patrick, our wiener dog, to visit, and he brings her chocolate. Plus, she isn't familiar with backpacking. Or the Appalachian Trail. I wouldn't need to share a whole lot of details because my mom had not been an outdoorsy-camping-hiker kind of woman. She liked her amenities, as I think did many people who lived through the depression. I can't say as I blame them. They met their challenges by day to day living. They didn't need to seek out activities that would leave them cold, hungry, and tired. They lived that already. Every single day.

Even though I committed to joining Julie on the AT, to strapping luggage to my back, even though I invested a considerable amount of money into proper equipment, I was still ambivalent. It wasn't that I didn't want to venture into the wilderness and maybe see rattlesnakes and bears; it was just that I was still having doubts about my ability to actually do this hike. I absolutely had some issues with my back. Running my fingers down my spine, I could feel the prominence of L4 and L5. My last x-ray stated: anterior slippage of L4 and 5. There is narrowing and increased sclerosis of the bilateral facet joints at L4 and L5. There is disc narrowing at L4 and L5, L5 and S1. The impression is grade 1 spondylolisthesis of L4 and 5 due to degenerative changes of the bilateral facet joints. Degenerative disc disease at L4 and 5, L5 and S1.

This report was from 2012, and probably I should have an

update, but honestly, I wasn't sure I really wanted to know. I am a fan of denial, and it seemed to be working for me. I didn't want to turn over a rock and actually find something unsettling. Better to just leave the rocks in place. If my symptoms should become more severe, I would move a rock.

Over the past year I chose to try and increase the strength of the muscles in my back which would subsequently increase my core strength. I gave in and went to the doctor during a really acute, painful period, and he ordered an anti-inflammatory and muscle relaxant. I hate to take strong medications, but I was desperate. Crawling on all fours was neither attractive nor efficient. Diclofenac and Cyclobenzaprine became my *friends*. Fortunately I responded quickly and didn't have to take them for very long.

My next doctor visit resulted in six weeks of physical therapy (PT) and a refill on the meds. The PT was marginally helpful, because most of the things they showed me, I already knew from my internet research. Still, I did pick up a few tips and new exercises. Forty plus years of running, mostly on pavement, in crap shoes, clearly had done some bad shit to my joints. I also had to admit, I was not in the "Kansas phase" of my life anymore. I had left Kansas and was heading for Appalachia.

I worried about my back a lot. I didn't want to resort to surgery because my internet research was not turning up good stuff pertaining to the back issues I was experiencing. Mostly, the surgery for my problem was done as a last resort, and I was certainly a long way from that station. Besides, I knew people who had undergone back surgery, and although some of them fared well, some did not. They did not see an improved lifestyle, and a few were even worse off. No. I wasn't ready for any surgery. Not now. Not yet. As long as I could do most of what I wanted to do physically, I saw no need to make any big changes. Since my internet sources, along with the docs and physical therapists, were telling me that core strength was what I needed, then core strength would be what I would get.

I began a daily regime of stretching, and I determined to get stronger, become more flexible, and defy this aging process that was ever so subtly and quite consistently reminding me, that quite frankly, the springtime of my life had blossomed, bloomed, and shriveled up. I was well into late summer, approaching fall.

That said, as much as I worked on getting stronger, worked on increasing my endurance, spent countless hours walking, added laps to my swim routine, I still worried that it wouldn't be enough. I fretted about wimping out on the first day of the hike. I would leave Julie in the woods, hitchhike back to my car, and slither home, a defeated, pain-racked wreck.

In addition to my orthopedic concerns, I also worried about my cardiac health. Over the years I experienced several episodes of arrhythmias and wore the twenty-four hour holter monitor on three different occasions. Once in my thirties, once in my forties, and once in my fifties I had those little electrodes stuck to my skin, giving me a rash and recording my heartbeats. Thankfully, nothing of substance was found, and I was basically told that stress was not my friend. The flutters I felt were benign and normal for me. Not to worry. The instructions were to do activities as tolerated and seek medical attention right away if I experienced shortness of breath, chest pain, or felt faint. The usual.

Actually, because I always led such an active life and general-ly did whatever I wanted, I forgot about the cardiac stuff. It had been awhile since I had noticed the flutters and because my back gave me so much discomfort (okay pain), all my other complaints were shelved for the time.

However, like any competent hypochondriac, which I admit to being, I could always conjure up a health problem to obsess over. I was a worrier. I was a chronic worrier. I began worrying at the age of ten when I browsed through my mother's medical encyclo-pedias and nursing books. When I was twelve I tripped on a diving board and broke my leg. The leg was pinned and cast to the thigh.

I spent three very long months in bed. Yes. Total bed rest. Bed-pans, bed baths, and turning sheets were my life. In my spare time, of which I had an abundance, I read my mother's medical books. She recently returned to school to become an LPN and had a menagerie of books about diseases, anatomy, pharmaceuticals, etc. There was a plethora of information all within reach of my bed, because books kept me occupied. When I was occupied I wasn't whining, crying, teasing, demanding, or being a general sassy little snot. Yes. My sweet mother actually called me that. More than once. When reminded about it today, she seems to have total amnesia. Since my bed had been set up in the dining room of our house, so that I wouldn't get lonely upstairs, my bad behavior affected everyone. Best to keep me busy. Books did the job. Keep the books coming. If I wanted my mom's nursing books, no problem. Were they appropriate for a twelve year old? Not so much.

I was a quick study regarding the medical information. I began wondering just how, with all of the things that could go wrong with a body, anyone could possibly be normal and disease-free. If only my schoolwork was as compelling to learn as the disease facts. Good or bad, I have retained much of that know-ledge today. Plus, I gained a whole lot more during the years I studied and then worked as a registered nurse. It's like my ex-husband's social security number. It is there. Imprinted into my brain like footprints in concrete. It ain't going away. Ever. I would love to store other facts up there, because I find myself often at a loss for thinking of a name, a place, or what I had to eat at the last meal. If I could just lose a few diseases and that social security number, I know I would be able to remember more names. And dates. And the reason I went to the store.

Since I am doing such an admirable job of owning up to my shortcomings, of which there do seem to be a significant number, I will also admit I am a pulse counter. Yes. I check my pulse. Fre-quently. Incessantly. Definitely abnormally. If I get a skipped beat, I get anxious. I mean, it isn't incapacitating anxiety, but it is there. I know that these are likely just harmless premature ventricular or atrial contractions, PVC's or PAC's, and because I am asymptomatic, I don't need to worry. I feel fine. I usually feel great. Still. I fret. I tell myself to take a couple of deep breaths, think about brownies and pizza. Sometimes this works; sometimes I just need to drink a glass of wine. Occasionally, I need to take a Valium. No. I am not proud of this quirky behavior.

"Sandy, I think you'll be fine. We'll go slow. I've been talking to people who have actually hiked on the trail, and they tell me that you average about two miles an hour. And we'll stop as much as we want," Julie would tell me reassuringly.

"Yeah, I know we can go slow. I just keep worrying about carrying all that weight. I'm really trying to keep my pack under twenty pounds. You know. Just take the bare essentials," I would reply.

Oh. My. What a silly girl. Twenty pounds. Really? What did I think I would be eating? Tree bark? Looking back, I totally understand why Julie didn't respond to my twenty pound pack absurdity. She was already practicing realistically. She would tell me about hiking ten miles with twenty pounds on her back plus water bottles.

"Wow," I would think. "I wonder why she's being so extreme? Why is she doing so much?"

Back in the days when we were training for our first marathon, I learned early that if I told her how far we would be running that day, she would just say that she couldn't do it. So, I began lying. I would tell her we would be running four miles, and we would go six. I would tell her eight miles, and we would run ten.

People are generally what I call distance-retarded. Well, perhaps the politically correct term is distance-impaired. It is difficult to ascertain distances unless you have experience. Runners and bikers are pretty good at it. Others are not. Julie was new at the running thing, and her distance impairment was clear. She had no idea. Gradually she caught on to my deceptions, but by the time she did, her endurance was good, and she had the confidence to run long distances. There was no way to deceive me like that during this hike training. Too bad. Maybe it would have helped me with my tepid confidence.

I don't know what I was thinking. If I just did the math, I would see that she was not extreme in the least. In fact, if anything, she was being conservative. The trail is a little over twenty-one hundred miles long. Plus, there is a seven mile approach trail that boasts six hundred and four steps. Think about it. Most thru-hikers take five to seven months to complete the trail, which means they would average ten to fourteen miles a day. That is pretty simple to calculate. Granted, we were just hiking a section, but still, we would likely be plodding along at a pace that would at least get us to a campground or shelter each day.

If I am to be perfectly honest here, I will admit that in all that time I spent thinking about, planning for, obsessing over, and talking about this hike, it never occurred to me to do this simple math and calculate how far we would be walking each day. I do not know what I was thinking, what alternate universe I was dwelling in, how naive I could be so as not to realize that in order to be ready for this type of physical activity, I actually had to practice walking more than two miles and carry a twenty pound pack.

Yes, I did practice a lot. I just didn't prepare adequately. I carried my backpack in the backseat of my car stuffed with my new sleeping bag, pad, a few clothing items, a couple packs of freeze-dried food, and a few incidentals. I got out of my car and walked around with it strapped on every chance I got. Can I just say, this was not even remotely adequate preparation? Doing just this seemed hard enough for me. It was a challenge with the fifteen pounds I was carrying. I knew how much it weighed, because I weighed it. And subsequently, I looked at the weight of everything that might be added to my pack. Those freeze dried packages of food? Did you know they came in different weights? The spaghetti weighed more than the scrambled eggs. We were only talking several ounces here, but still, it all added up. An ounce here, an ounce there, and pretty soon, there was yet another pound to be toted.

Carrying the twenty-one pound bag of kitty litter into my house one afternoon really got my attention. I could not imagine carrying that monster on my back. One day, after spreading out everything I could possibly imagine needing onto the bed, and then stuffing it into the pack, hoisting it onto my back, strapping it in place, and walking around the yard (Around the yard??? Really?? Like that was any kind of hiking preparation???), I decided to just be done with it. I was ready. I would worry about the water bottles later. Actually, maybe I could just strap them to my waist. That would keep my pack lighter. Yes. That would be my plan. Like Scarlet O'Hara in *Gone with the Wind*, at the end of the movie, when she didn't know how she would be getting Rhett back, and said, "I'll think about that tomorrow."

I would do the same. I would think about my heavy pack and the AT later. Meanwhile, I would keep practicing in the very non-exerting way I had been doing. I'd walk around the house, the yard, up the road a mile. I'd loop the water bottles to a belt, and I would aim to get my distance up to three miles. Clearly, I was writing the handbook on how *not* to prepare for hiking the Appalachian Trail. Looking back, what I should have done, was go to the YMCA with my pack fully loaded, strap that baby into place, climb up on the grueling, torturous stair-climber, and spend a few hours.

I will, however, give myself credit for consistency. My training may have been sorely inadequate, but if nothing else, it was consistent. Every day while at work, I would spend my lunch time, which was a whopping thirty minutes, hiking the perimeter of the campus. Figuring that the slight inclines served as the hills I would be facing, I actually felt quite smug. Admittedly, I also liked the attention it got for me. I enjoyed strapping on the pack and telling people about my hiking trip, which I would be starting shortly after my impending date of retirement. People would sort of *ooh and ahh*. At least that was my impression of their reactions. Looking back, it was likely more of a *better you than me* reaction. Some women actually cringed when they asked me about where I would shower at the end of the day. I told them I wouldn't be showering or bathing at all. Conveying that information usually produced a curled lip and slightly audible, "Ewwww."

Every day, for my last month of work, at 11:20 AM, I strapped on the pack, put on my safari hat, and plodded out my office door, hoping to encounter questions and comments. Yes. It is amazing to think that a sixty-one year old woman who had run three marathons, biked across the northeast and around the Gaspe Peninsula could actually believe that walking around a mostly flat campus for thirty minutes with a fifteen pound pack strapped on would be adequate training to tackle the terrain of Pennsylvania in heat and humidity. Silly girl. Silly, foolish, naive girl.

Chapter 6: Day of Departure: For me

Once Julie actually left town with her brother, headed to Harpers Ferry, where she would begin her hike, I really turned up the training routine. At least I thought I was turning it up. I was now absolutely determined not to wimp out on the first day. She planned to hike the first three days with her brother, Bruce, also known as Broom, the explanation for which would likely require another book. Suffice it to say, Brother Bruce/Broom would help her get started, and then after she'd gone about one hundred miles, I would join her. We had joked about this because Bruce did not practice, did not train, did absolutely nothing to prepare himself for walking ten plus miles a day through the woods with forty pounds on his back. Yes, he carried most of the food, which added the weight.

I have met Bruce. And, I have seen him recently. He smokes, eats junk food and it would be a stretch to say he weighs one hundred forty pounds. He does not belong to a gym. So far as I know, he has never visited one. Ever. He is very, very thin, and his idea of hiking gear was a Walmart tent, food, water, cigarettes, a lighter and matches. His clothing would be work boots, blue jeans, and his cowboy hat. Bruce is a good guy. He loves nature. He isn't much of a planner regarding amenities needed on a hiking trail. He has determination. And, attitude.

Once Bruce left, Julie would call me when she got near Boiling Springs, Pa. According to the Appalachian Trail Guide, the bible for all AT hikers, this was a relatively flat section and very scenic. Since I was only planning on being a short term section hiker, the idea of flat terrain was very appealing. Had Julie and I studied the guide just a little closer, we would have noticed that yes, indeed the Boiling Springs area was flat, but it was also short. Maybe ten miles, tops. Then the trail became rougher. OK. It got really rough. Steep, rocky, and tough. Of course, I considered none of those things. I gave no thought to steep, rocky, and tough.

I thought only of flat, pretty, tree-lined, bubbling brooks, cold streams, and beautiful, sunny weather, accompanied by cool breezes. Silly girl. Silly, stupid girl.

It appears that for me, history is not a very good teacher. Or, maybe she teaches well but I just don't pay attention. I am a poor student. In 2002, Julie and I decided to take a bike trip around the Gaspe Peninsula, where the St. Lawrence River empties into the Atlantic Ocean. I chose the route because it followed the coast. That meant it would essentially be flat. Right? Like walking along the beach? I never consulted a topographical map. The route was not at all flat. Ever. Saying the hills were brutal is an understatement. Not only did we push our bikes up mountains, but we walked them down as well. They were too steep to trust our brakes. We completed our trip, which included road grades of seventeen percent, but I don't know how we managed.

I would follow Julie's Facebook posts every day and message her that I was ready anytime. I could do hills, no problem. I based that assertion on the one time walk I took up our paved road with my twenty-ish pound pack. The distance covered was about two miles. The fact that I could walk around our house for an hour on the uneven lawn told me that I was ready for whatever challenging terrain the trail had to offer. Bring on the AT! I was ready! I would rock it! I. Was. Clueless.

"Jule, I'm ready. Really. I don't need to wait for you to get to Boiling Springs. The hills won't be a problem. My back has been fine," I messaged her after she had been gone about five days.

And I anxiously waited for her response. On the evening of July 5th, the phone rang.

"Sandy, I have the perfect place for you to meet me. I'll be in Caledonia State Park tomorrow afternoon. Can you come?" asked Julie.

"Jule! OMG! I am so ready! My pack's loaded and in the car! I've got a water bottle carrier to wear around my waist so I don't have to add all that extra weight to my back," I said so so excitedly, completely oblivious to the fact that the carrier itself weighed a pound, and the spiffy new bottles I'd purchased were not exactly lightweight. Nice. Sturdy. Not lightweight.

"And I'll bring our dinner. How about some watermelon? And fresh fruit? I've got a couple of those small bottles of champagne so we can toast our new adventure. What time should I get there?"

"Anytime in the afternoon. I'll be here. That fresh fruit sure does sounds good! Eating on the trail is pretty shitty. I can't believe I'm not constipated. Must be all the walking helps," said Julie

"Oh, and do you have a tent? Something bigger than this mini one I have? If you do, bring it. We can sprawl out for at least one night here in the campground," suggested Julie.

I did have a big tent. It was like a bedroom. A king-sized bed, dresser, and chair would have comfortably fit in the thing. We bought it a couple of years ago, planning to do a lot of camping. We used it once. John's oldest granddaughter used it once. Yes. I definitely had a large tent to sprawl out in Caledonia State Park.

Giving John last minute instructions on cat care for our very elderly felines with very poor litter box aim, I made some last minute adjustments to my gear.

"John, remember, you have to scoop out the litter every day. They pee a ton, and it's a big mess if you wait a few days. You won't like it. And pet them. Talk baby talk to them like I do. You know, the way you do to Patrick. (Our wiener dog. John's boy. John's boy who I am pretty sure he loves more than me.) And when you visit my mother, remember to take her chocolate. Check her Depends supply, too. I think I stocked her up alright, but just check, OK?"

Yes. I know. My husband is sort of saintly. Scooping kitty litter and keeping due vigilance of personal care items for my mom is above the call of duty. I always tell him, that's why I picked him! I mean, I could have married any number of men that second time around. Well, maybe not any number. Possibly one. But still. I picked him. Maybe he dressed a little more casually that I would like, wasn't especially punctual, made a mess of the kitchen on those rare occasions when he cooked, and didn't like my taste in TV sitcoms, but he sure was a kind man. I loved him. He has been my constant, my rock, for the past twenty-seven years.

It would be about a five hour drive to Caledonia State Park. I am not much for listening to the radio in the car because it seems I can never find a station playing the music I want to hear, or radio shows talking about topics that hold my interest. Yeah, National Public Radio is good, but so often, when I am ready to listen, they are playing classical music. That's all very nice. I enjoy classical music. At bedtime. I don't need to be drowsy when I'm driving.

Therefore, I always, always, always have an audio book, or two, or three in the car. I have listened to hundreds over the years. I have my favorite authors, and often I will just get a book I have already read (listened to). I find that it's like watching reruns on TV. I have my favorites and an amazing tolerance for repeat performances. This makes John crazy. He's not a big sitcom fan to begin with and hearing the whistling from The Andy Griffin Show over and over and over again, sort of gets on his every last nerve. There's no yelling. Just silence and then he leaves the room. He mumbles. The laugh track drones on, I am transported back to the 50's, John grabs a book, or goes to his man-cave, and we live in peace.

I would be checking out a new author and reader on my long drive through Pennsylvania. A friend raved to me about *The Outlander* series by Diana Gabaldon. The local public library happened to carry this in audio, and the first book was available. What the hell. I checked it out along with one of my old stand-by favorites, just in case I couldn't get interested in this new series. It was historical fiction, which I do generally like. *Gone with the Wind* is one of my all-time favorite books. I have read it once, listened to the audio version twice, and lost track of the number of times I've seen the movie. Yes. Historical fiction, for me, is very good.

So. My bag was packed, my car loaded, instructions left for John, animals petted, mom's personal care arsenal stocked. My car pointed south. Before I was out of the driveway, the CD player of my car turned on, and I was hearing about WWII in England. The sun shone, temperatures were predicted to climb into the nineties, and I was freed from all drudgery of household chores for at least a week. I was committing to eating shitty processed food, filtering my water from streams, sleeping with my girlfriend (not girlfriend like in lesbian romance, but girlfriend like in school) in a tiny tent, stinking because I couldn't bathe, and performing all manner of toilet type functions in the woods. Behind a bush. Or in a hole. With no toilet paper, because I decided to cut weight and use leaves. Nice. Why was I so excited about this? But oh, I was so very excited! I was giddy!

About two hours into my drive and several chapters into my book, the phone rang.

"Mom, how's your trip? When do you leave?" asked Jamie, my daughter.

"Hi honey. Well, I'm actually on my way. I still can't really believe I'm doing this. How's everything up in Buffalo-town?"

"I'm fine. Actually, I'm calling with bad news," she began.

Great. I'm not even one day away from home, and I get bad news. Panic ran through me. My heart started to race like it can when the phone rings in the middle of the night. No one ever calls at three AM just to chat. That are calling to tell you something very bad. Something that can't wait until morning. Something that must begin being dealt with right then. In the middle of the night. And if someone calls during daylight hours and starts the conversation off with "I have some bad news," brace for impact; it ain't likely to be pretty.

"I didn't want you to see it on Facebook or have gramma call you wondering what happened. I just wanted you to know that our cousin, Robin, died. I'm not sure who Robin is, but there were all sorts of messages on Facebook. Did she go to the reunions?" asked Jamie.

"OMG! What happened? Robin isn't that old. And, yeah. She was always at the reunions. She's the one from Australia," I answered.

"Near as I can tell from the postings, she fell down the stairs and hit her head," said Jamie.

"Oh my God! That's so horrible! I'll let gramma know. Thanks for telling me now," I said.

"I wasn't sure if I should tell you, but figured you'd see it as soon as you checked your phone. And don't worry about gramma; I'll call and check on her while you're gone. I know John's going over, too," said Jamie.

"OK. Well, I guess that really cements another reason why I'm doing this hike. We just never know, right? Do it while you can. Live in the moment," I tried to be philosophical.

"Yeah. Say hi to Julie. And have fun! This is so cool that you're doing this!"

I clicked the hang-up button on my steering column, turned my book back on, and continued driving south. Thinking about my cousin, I felt a moment of appreciation for being able to take this trip, and I considered my own mortality. This was no time for a pulse check. I quickly tuned back into my book because I did not want to start obsessing about my health issues, real or imagined. I. Just. Wanted. To. Hike. In. The. Woods. And be fine about not bathing. This was something I *could* do. Now. I just needed to embrace the opportunity.

Following the death call from my daughter, the rest of the drive, thankfully, was uneventful. Until I got to Caledonia State Park. And, I have to say, I did almost miss the turn for that. Pennsylvania obviously does not invest the same amount of money into road signs that New York does. In New York, whenever there is an attraction coming up, there are multiple appropriately spaced signs advertising this. It was a good thing I had a map, in addition to my GPS, because regarding the Caledonia State Park signs, they were pretty sparse. There was one. Uh huh. Just one. And that was about a mile from the park entrance. There was nothing on the highway, nothing when I got off the highway, nothing until I made the last turn that my GPS told me to do.

Finding the entrance to the park, I turned in. There was no place to pay, though. That seemed odd. I was pretty sure this wasn't a free deal. This certainly wouldn't be happening in New York State. Our state park entrances are so well fortified that an armed guard wouldn't seem out of place. I kept driving and tried calling Julie to tell her I was here, but there was no cell signal. OK. No problem. How big could the park be? I would just drive around the campground loops until I found her. That should be easy enough. Look for the campsite with no car.

While driving around, my new phone, which can I just say I barely could operate, having just cashed in my old flip phone for this Samsung thing, buzzed. The salesman gave us a crash course of sorts, but it was proving sorely inadequate for my needs. Hmm. Buzz. That must mean a message. Sure enough, I checked my texts, and Julie had sent me her campsite number. Ahh. That would certainly make finding her easy. One would think, right? Except that when I toured the loop where her number should be, her number was not there. There was no indication of any other campsites in the area. Shit. Fuck. Damn. I tried calling. No signal. More shit. Fuck. Damns.

Then another text popped up. She said she had to change sites and gave me another number. Hmmm. What to do? I remembered when I entered the park that there was actually another entrance up about a mile from the first one, which I had discovered when I overshot it. Driving out of the park, I made the turn to go up to the other entrance and pulled in. Spotting the loop for campsites, I slowly drove around it, and voila! There was Julie!

"Jule! Girlfriend! Wow! One hundred miles! You're here!"

We hugged and didn't exactly jump up and down, but certainly were excited enough to do just that.

"I know! Can you believe it? And you won't believe what's happened today. It's like I am in some sort of witness protection program," began Julie.

"I was so exhausted when I got here. And I got screwed up on the trail and had to walk an extra couple miles, which I didn't need because I was so exhausted. I felt like shit. Anyhow, I got my tent set up and showered. Sandy, I smelled so bad. I mean really. I could barely stand the smell of myself. It was horrible. You name it. Rotten crotch, smelly armpits, stale urine. I was worse than any stinky labor patient we ever had. That shower just felt so good. And then this morning, a van packed with people stopped in front of my campsite, and some guy started taking pictures. Of me, I guess," Julie explained.

"You mean he got right out of the van?" I asked.

"No, but he rolled down the window and held out the phone. You could tell he was taking pictures. It kind of creeped me out. And then a few hours later, the van was back, and the guy took more pictures. This time one of the campground staff saw it, and she came over to me after the van left. She told me she had gotten the license plate number and was reporting it to camp security, which made me feel a little better, but it sort of scared me, too."

"So what did they do? Has the van come back?"

"The security guy was so nice. He came out to my site and told me they were moving me. That's why we have this place in the RV part with the electric hook up, which is so good, because we can charge our phones. And look at all this firewood! We can have a campfire!"

She's right, I recall thinking to myself. That would be very creepy. And a bit unsettling. Interesting though, as she was explaining her saga of the day, the mention of the word campfire was what got my attention most. What the hell? What kind of bitch-friend was I? And what was she thinking? The temperature peaked out in the mid nineties and probably cooled down to a balmy eighty-nine after the sun went down. Why would we want to sit in front of a blazing campfire in that heat? Was she asking for the mother of all hot flashes? Besides, I hadn't brought marshmallows, so there would be no s'mores. What good is a campfire without s'mores? I didn't want to pull a Nancy Negative here, so I tried to feign as much enthusiasm for her campfire idea, as the concern I genuinely felt for her unwanted photo op. Plus, now that I was here, the errant van had my attention, too.

"The security guy, Tom, told me that they are pretty sure they're homeless people who just came into the park to shower. They weren't checked in, but they'd seen the van before. He assured me now that they had the description and the license number, they'd be looking for it and would be calling the police," Julie continued.

"Since we've been moved to the other side of the park, I registered under a different name. Did you notice it said Burr on the sign marking my site? I mean, I've been using my maiden name where I can but since my divorce still isn't final, I can't do it for legal things. Anyway, they changed the name, and hopefully the van won't be back. I do feel better now that you're here, and we have a car parked at our site. I'm sure the fact that I'm a woman and alone with no car made me some sort of easy target. Can you just imagine how freaked out the girls back home would be at this?" laughed Julie.

"I know. I can't imagine any of the girls, or guys for that matter, who would want to be doing this. You know how it goes. They want to shop, go for lunch, and see a movie. Maybe take in a ballgame. What people our age would want to pee in the woods and stink? Not change their underwear! Can you think of anyone? Pussies! All of them!" I added, and laughed out loud.

"Well, all I can say, is this has been one hell of a trip, and I'm not even two weeks into it! We sure are going to have stories for the grandkids. And the staff at the *home!*" said Julie.

Whenever we had an adventure, we would talk about gathering footage for the mental movies we'd play when we were old. I joked about telling my daughter that if she ever put me in a *home*, I would be very naughty.

She'd be getting calls daily with the staff telling her, "Jamie, we just don't know if we can keep your mother here. She causes so many problems. Did you know that she organized a demonstration and led a group of wheelchairs through the kitchen because she claims the food isn't healthy? She says it's processed and has too many preservatives. She keeps demanding a glass of wine every afternoon, but we just can't mix alcohol with the medications she's taking. And she has all those political signs in her room. We've told her she can't keep using tape because it pulls the paint and wallpaper off. Now she's telling us that if we don't get better entertainment she will pee on the floor outside of her room. You've got to talk to her," I explained, trying to keep a straight face.

Some of the shit I told her was made up. But some of it actually happened to me back in the days when I worked on a geriatric hospital floor. Never underestimate a mature mind. Those sweet-looking old folks can be devious.

"I know, I try not to think about it. Can you imagine if we were actually roommates in the *home*?" said Julie. We both knew a good deal about the *home*. My mother has been in assisted living since 2009, and Julie spent the past ten years working in a long term care facility. We were well acquainted with the antics of the elderly. Old did not mean quiet, complacent, and cooperative.

We made a lot of mind movie reels over the years. Dating, divorces, re-marriages, bike trips, crossing an international bridge on our bikes, white water rafting, downhill skiing, x-country skiing topless, three days of fame in Gloucester after the first bike trip, labor and delivery stories, health scares, career changes, the list just goes on and on. Several years ago I introduced Julie to my college roommates, Rox and Nancy. We still try to have our "girls weekend" every year, and it is always like no time has passed. We quickly revert back to our roles as roomies in the seventies. We are all twenty again. I knew that Julie would fit right into this mix. She certainly has. She is now considered a "roomie," and is included in all of our gatherings.

A woman once told me that at the end of your life you would be very fortunate if you could count all of your really good friends on one hand. These are the people that you could call in the middle of the night at any time, and say, "Can you come? I really need you," and they would be there. At the time, I didn't really think much about that because it seemed I had so very many friends. Looking back, I really didn't. I knew a lot of people. I didn't have a lot of really good friends. Not the *call in the middle of the night* kind of friend. Julie, Rox, and Nancy are all *call in the middle of the night* girls. Julie would be bringing her strength, her pragmatism. Rox would come along with her sense of humor and positive attitude, and Nancy would bring kindness along with the food and wine.

Settled into our campsite for the night with phones plugged nicely into the power outlets, campfire sizzling because we couldn't seem to get it going very well, we kicked back, literally, in the folding chairs I pulled from the back of Lucy. At this point we didn't know that Purell was an excellent fire starter. We would learn about that in a couple of days at Birch Run Shelter. I have to say, I wasn't very sorry that the thing sizzled because I was just so freaking hot. What would I do tomorrow? On the trail? With my heavy pack? And my long pants, long sleeves, and hat to protect my damaged skin?

I did not sleep well that first night in the campground at Caledonia State Park. I suppose I shouldn't have expected to sleep well. I sleep like shit at home in my comfy bed, cuddled next to my husband. Why would I expect to sleep well on the ground with nothing but a flat half inch of padding between me and the dirt? Julie did. How do I know? I mean other than asking, "Hey, how'd you sleep?" I know because I laid awake for what seemed like most of the night, and I listened to her snore. Plus, it seems that my need to pee in the night is directly proportional to convenience of said peeing. If it is extremely inconvenient, like maybe I am sleeping on a top bunk, or crammed next to the wall (I think I am supposed to say bulkhead when referring to walls of a boat) in the V-berth of our sailboat, and have to climb over John, locate Patrick Wiener Dog and not squash him, I will invariably need to pee at least three times in an eight hour time span. If it is raining and I need to walk to the clubhouse of the marina, likely it will be four times. At home, where our bedroom is connected to the bathroom, I may need to pee once. Or I will make it through an entire night with no bathroom visit.

Because our tent was located some distance from the bathroom, of course my bladder was on hyper alert. I think I remember four trips. Maybe more. All I really recall of that first night, once our campfire finally totally fizzled out, was Julie's snoring, me needing to pee, and being so freaking hot that I actually considered getting up and taking a cold shower. I hoped this was not a prelude to what lay ahead on the trail. I certainly wanted more exciting and enjoyable mental movie footage than this.

I finally fell asleep sometime just after dawn. Of course. Just like at home. I toss and turn most of the night, fret about my alarm going off at 5:30 AM, and enter into my deep sleep phase at 5 AM. Also, this new self-inflating mattress that I paid way too much for in the camping store proved to be very insufficient. I would have had more padding with a towel. Worthless plastic piece of shit is what came to mind as I tossed and turned all night, feeling every stone, stick, and blade of grass under me. I still woke up before Julie, and again, I know this, because the snoring continued.

Hmmm. Did she snore like this on the bike trips? Did I just sleep better back then because I was premenopausal and just didn't know? I think I would have remembered epic snoring like this.

Oh well. Not much to do about it other than get up in the night and push her over on her side if this continued on the hike. That little tent of hers was tiny. Any snoring would be maddening.

Thankfully, I didn't snore. Or, did I?? Naw. John would have told me. But then, come to think of it, how would he know? The man falls asleep as he's reaching to turn off the light. I mean, he hits the bed, his head touches the pillow, and he has entered the land of somnolence. He can fall asleep anytime, anywhere. And, yes. He snores. Loudly. So really, I should feel quite at home in the tent on the trail. Right?

Chapter 7: First Day on the Trail: Thursday, July 7, 2016

Talking excitedly about our upcoming day over our breakfast of granola, fruit, nuts, coffee (for Julie), tea (for me), and juice, I already was sweating. It was more of a breakfast for birds than of champions. But it was what we had. There would be no eggs and toast on the trail. Of course we relished taking showers because we did not anticipate being clean for the next week unless we found a deep stream or got rained on.

I couldn't find my bra. I knew I packed one because I remember thinking that if it got really, really hot, I could just wear that. I know that would not be an attractive sight. Although I am still pretty thin and I have weighed one hundred twenty-five to one hundred thirty pounds for a long time, things don't really look that good, unless I am viewed from a distance. There is no six-pack, although I can't remember when there ever was. Still, I don't recall the amount of flab and jiggly stuff around my middle that has taken up permanent residency there now. Of course, I have to admit to the sun damaged crepey skin that is now mine, too. No. Me in just a sports bra wouldn't be pretty.   But then, who cares? It's not like I am ever going to see the people who pass by me on the trail again. Right? And Julie won't care because she may be in her sports bra, too. Yes, she looks better than I do, but not much. She's also got the sixty year old body workin' for her. Beauty queens, we are not.

I needed to find that bra. I tore through my gym bag, my back pack, and throughout my car. No bra. Shit. It was time to improvise. Here I was, not even on the trail yet, and already problem solving by creating something new out of something old. Taking one of the multiple bathing suits stuffed into my gym bag and locating my bandage cutting scissors, which I had just known would be needed on the hike, I cut off the top part of a bathing suit. Voila!

"Jule, check it out! What do you think? This is my new

sports bra!" I said, holding it up, proudly displaying my creative handiwork that was obviously cut at an angle. Yes. Crooked.

"Sandy, that is just beautiful. I can't wait to see you in it," replied Julie, with what I recognized as total sarcasm.

OK. So, it wouldn't make me an underwear model. Maybe I didn't exactly cut very straight. Hey, bandage scissors were not made to cut cloth. I thought I had done alright. What the hell. It was better than nothing. I may not look all that good in just a sports bra, but I can honestly say I sure look better than topless. And I look a whole lot better than some of my age mates!

By 10 AM we were packed with all of the extraneous gear stowed away in Lucy, my car. At this point, Lucy was very, very full. We still needed to get a parking permit and move her to a parking lot on the far side of the park because we couldn't leave her at the campsite once we checked out. Julie suggested we leave our packs with some other campers when we moved her because we would be walking more than a mile back to our original site in order to get onto the trail. There was no point in carrying those packs any further than we needed. Already, the temperature was in the mid-eighties, and it was very humid.

Looking around at the camping neighbors, we immediately ruled out the entourage closest to us. They had multiple dogs, which was fine, except the dogs seemed to be fighting with each other most of the time. They growled, yelped, yipped and barked. Their owners, at least I assumed they were the owners, kept yelling at them to "Shut up." Nice. They reminded me of folks you might see on The Judge Judy Show. Or, maybe Jerry Springer. No. We wouldn't ask them to keep our packs. We decided on a young couple to the left of us. It was apparent they weren't check-ing out that day because they had an elaborate set-up and were sprawled out comfortably.

We introduced ourselves, dropped off the packs, and drove to the park office to obtain our long term parking permit. That was accomplished with no problem. As we were leaving the office

Julie recognized a couple of hikers she had met on the trail. It is trail custom to get a trail name and only use that. No one introduces themselves by their full names. Sometimes you choose your own name. But generally, as other hikers meet up with you on the trail, spend time with you in the shelters, and observe your behavior, they choose a name they think fits you. Usually this happens very early into the hike. All of the shelters have logs that hikers sign when they leave and also write their comments. Only trail names are used.

"Oh my God! I remember you guys! Hash Brown and The Natural, right? And your dog is Maple Syrup! That night in the shelter with you guys was so amazing! I was so tired and when you offered to share your dinner with me, that was just so nice! You know, that has been my best night on the trail so far," said Julie.

"Sandy, these are the guys I slept in the shelter with. Remember when I told you about how they cooked for me and all?"

She then introduced me and explained that I was joining her for a week on the trail. The thing I remember most about them was how very, very thin they were. The dog was husky enough, but these guys looked like a day away from Auschwitz. Also, one of them was wearing a skirt. Maybe it was actually a kilt, but whatever, it was a dress-like thing. I'll bet it was cooler than wearing pants. Or, maybe he had lost his pants. I didn't ask. Now, I wish I had. At the time it seemed like it would be rude.

When we were out of earshot, she whispered that they had also shared their "pot" with her. She attributes the good night's sleep she got with them to the fact that she was stoned.

"I hadn't had pot since the seventies. Other than the brownie I ate that time with you and John. It was pretty nice," said Julie.

Yes. This lucky bitch was the only girl in a bedroom full of men, because that's all shelters are, just one big bedroom. Sixty years old and she'd had a pajama party and gotten stoned with men who were under the age of forty. They even cooked for her. Seriously, does it get any better? Even though she had only been on the trail for a week, she already experienced fellowship, community, and illegal drugs with other hikers. They watched out for each other. They shared. That, for me, was reassuring. I wondered what our trail names would be. And I wondered if I would get to smoke any pot.

Walking back to our campsite to pick up the packs was pleasant enough, even though it was already sweltering and sticky. Overdressed in my hiker pants, long sleeved shirt that I chose because I wanted to limit the sun damage to my arms, and my safari hat, I was managing well enough. I was hot, but I had been hotter. Julie wore shorts and a short sleeved shirt. I remember thinking she would be getting more sun damage than I would. She also would be way more comfortable. Already, I was dripping. And I didn't even have my pack.

Supposedly it was only a mile from the office back to our campsite. I am a pretty good judge of distance, and all I can say is that was one long mile. Julie got directions to where we would pick up the trail. Retrieving our packs, strapping them on, posing for a photo op, we were ready to go. I was actually going to start hiking on the Appalachian Trail! I was going to sleep in the woods in a teeny tent! Yes! Bring it on! Maybe I would even see a bear!

I have to say that carrying that full pack, even with the water bottles flopping at my waist seemed to be OK. As I mentioned before, I am a pulse counter, and when Julie was looking the other way, trying to figure out whether we were indeed going in the right direction, I gave a quick check. No worry. I was fine. I was just sweating a lot. I mean, I was really, really sweating a lot. One would think that this would have been a good time to roll up my pants and change out the long sleeved shirt for something cooler. Losing the hat would have been a wise choice as well.

"Jule, aren't you hot?" I asked.

"Not bad. I'm dressed a little cooler than you are. Are you

sure you don't want to change?"

"No. I'm good. I don't want to get too much sun, you know?" I explained.

"Well, I got pretty hot last week. It felt better to just wear the cooler clothes. There isn't that much sun when you get in the woods," she told me.

She should have conveyed that message in stronger language. Something like, "Are you fucking nuts dressed in all that shit? You'll roast!" would have been good. But, she didn't.

I did, however, ponder her suggestion. Then I thought of the wrinkly skin on my forearms. And legs. A lot on my face. And, I pulled the brim of my safari hat down and maintained maximum coverage from my shirt and pants. Plus, I didn't want to get insect bites. After all, we hear so much about Lyme disease, I sure didn't want to risk getting that. Yes. Better to sweat and drink some extra water. I would be fine. I was so very, very stupid. What was I thinking? I did not seem to be adequately processing just exactly how hot and humid it was. The sun damage to my skin had already been done. That ship had sailed, train left the station, road already traveled, whatever term I wanted to apply here fit. The point being, that my skin had long ago reached the point of no youthful return. Anything I did from now until I died was simply damage control, and it was minimal control at that. Perhaps I subconsciously overdressed to see just how close I could come to suffering from heat exhaustion. Stupid woman!

We continued walking up the road searching for a white blaze mark on a tree. The Appalachian Trail is marked by small white rectangles, two by six inches, painted periodically on trees, rocks, or posts. Following these correctly will keep any fool on the trail. Getting lost out here would actually be a challenge. And, we would be meeting that challenge soon enough. Julie was given directions from the ranger who claimed to know where the trail intersected the park. Since her campsite was moved from the first night, she wasn't exactly sure where she came into the park. Several miles up the road, with no indication of any blazes, both dripping with perspiration and likely beginning to stink, we sat down on a log at the side of the road. Julie pulled out her Appalachian Trail guide.

"Hmmmm. We should have found the trail by now. I'm wondering if that ranger guy sent us the wrong way. I'm going up ahead to look around. Why don't you just wait here with our packs?" Julie suggested.

No problem for me. I am no hero. I don't know shit about what to look for, and I was freaking hot. I didn't argue. Here I was, sweat pouring off me like I'm standing in a shower, and we hadn't even found the trail. However, this would be an excellent opportunity to check my pulse. Whew. Still OK. When did I turn into this wretch of a hypochondriac? I really needed to let the pulse thing go. Or, get medicated for obsessive-compulsive behavior. Not thinking I was quite that bad, I vowed to do less checking. Unless I wasn't feeling well. Then it would be totally OK. I would actually be prudent, right? She was gone about fifteen minutes.

"I think we need to go back. This doesn't seem right," she announced.

Right about then a car pulled up next to us, and two older men, both smoking pipes, got out and asked us if we were OK. Now when I say older, it just means not really young. I don't want to refer to my age mates as older, because that makes me old. I am having enough trouble with this concept as it is. So, maybe I should just say two gentlemen in the age range of fifty to eighty. Sometimes it's difficult to really tell a person's age. Suffice it to say, these pipe smokers were a bit past their prime. If I had to guess, I would say they were seventyish. Which, come to think of it, is not much older than we are.

They were very nice, very solicitous. We asked them if they knew how to access the AT. They both answered that indeed they did, and we were heading in the wrong direction.

We were told we needed to go back to the park, actually the part where the swimming pool was located. That happened to be the area where we left Lucy parked. It was a good couple of miles back, and I have to say, I was not looking forward to the walk. Shit. I would be spending the entire first day of my hike just trying to find the trail. I would be exhausted before my feet ever hit the thing.

"Would you guys mind driving us back to the park?" I asked, quite boldly, I might add.

"Sure, we can do that. We can't all fit what with your packs and our fishing gear, though. Bob won't mind waiting here," said the driver.

"I'm Larry, and this is Bob." Larry made the introduction as he rearranged the fishing gear in the back of the car.

Bob seemed totally fine with giving up his seat, as he continued puffing contentedly on his pipe. OK. So. I know what you're probably thinking. How could two women be so naive as to take a ride from a couple of strangers out in a wooded, semi-secluded area? Who knew what they might do? Right? All I can say is that sometimes in life you just have to take a chance. Listen to your gut, pull out all of your well-developed people reading skills, and just take a chance. If it seems like a good idea, it probably is. And, this definitely had all the ingredients of a good idea. They were willing; we were hot, sweaty, and lost. No way did we want to walk all the way back to the park. Larry was very cordial, telling us he is retired military, a widower who remarried, and whose wife didn't like him picking up hikers, which he often did anyway. He told us he felt like that was doing a good deed, and he planned to keep right on doing it. Nice for us! I suspected that he would not be telling his wife about today's pick up.

Dropping us off in the parking lot, actually not far from where Lucy sat, he pointed us toward the nearest blaze. Thanking him, we strapped the packs on, gulped some water, and headed north. Except that we didn't. Turns out Larry did know where the trail came into the park, he just had his directions reversed. About one quarter of a mile underway, having seen my first trail blaze, Julie stopped to check her compass.

"We need to turn around. Larry pointed us south, and we need to go north," said Julie.

Sounded good to me. What did I know? At this point, I didn't care. Because I was now hiking on the Appalachian Trail! Me! Sixty-one years old with a twenty-five plus pound pack, two liters of water dangling from my waist, along with a belly bag stuffed with food. I was doing it. I had this thing. It was mine. I owned it. Well. Maybe.

Less than a mile in the proper direction, we came to a hill. It was a very, very steep hill, with large stone steps made from boulders. I do mean steep. I had not practiced for this. And I had not anticipated so steep, so soon. Maybe I would be owning nothing here.

"Holy shit! This is a fucking mountain!" I gasped.

"Yeah, it is kind of steep. Don't worry. You'll be fine. We can stop as much as we need to. Remember, no hurry here," said Julie reassuringly.

I don't like to think of myself as a wimp. I am willing to try new things, attempt new challenges. But this was one mother-fucker of a mountain! Yes. I tend to curse a lot when I am challenged. I did the same thing on the bike trips when we climbed the mountains. Swearing got me up the hills. I suppose there are some folks who would stop and pray. Not me. I just curse. The steeper the hill, the greater the amount of profanity. And as I recalled, Julie certainly spewed forth her share on the mountains of those bike trips. Actually, if I am to be honest here, I have to admit that I just plain curse a lot, period. Trash mouth. That's me.

Except, now she wasn't cursing. Breathing heavy, but not cursing. No problem. I could cover us both. About ten minutes into the climb, I was panting, puffing, dripping, and really concerned that I might actually suffer a heart attack right here. Right on the first climb.

"I need to rest," I wheezed, as I plopped down on a rock.

"Holy shit! Have you climbed many of these this past week?" I asked.

"Yeah, some were pretty bad. They were longer and steeper than this is. You just get used to it," said Julie.

Looking at her, I noticed she wasn't dripping like I was. But then, I suppose my long sleeves, pants, and hat weren't helping any. Assessing the rate at which I was perspiring and doing a quick pulse check, because at this point it seemed very wise, I made the decision to cut my losses on the sun damage. I needed to cool off.

Rolling my pants up to capris length and fastening the little buttons on each side of the pant leg was my first step. Then up went the sleeves of my shirt, and off came the hat. I was still sweating, but it did feel a little better. Even a warm breeze on wet skin is refreshing.

"I think you're going to feel better. I wondered how long you were going to keep wearing all that shit. That's why I'm dressed like this. I started out with all that and just about died. It's just too hot out here," said Julie.

"What's your pulse like? Do you ever check it? Do you ever worry?" I asked.

"I don't check. When it pounds so hard it feels like it's coming out of my chest, I sit down."

"Oh," I said.

"Do you mind if we sit here for a few minutes?" I asked.

"Sit as long as you need to. Remember, we have all afternoon. We'll be fine."

I was ready to continue the climb after about fifteen minutes, and there were several more rest stops before we reached the top. Sadly, I have to confess, I bitched, whined, and swore most of the way. I was even annoying to myself.

Finally, just before the trail leveled out, Julie turned to me and said, very clearly, "Sandy. You're ruining my trip. There are going to be lots more hills. Whining doesn't help. Do you know who you sound just like? Yeah. *Her*. What's happened to you? When did you get so negative?"

Whoa. She totally and completely had my attention. What was I doing? The *her* she mentioned referenced a very irritating woman we both knew who whined incessantly. I hated whining. Julie was right. I was not only on the way to ruining the trip for her, but for me as well. This behavior was not who I was. At this moment in time, I didn't recognize me either.

"Jule, you're right. I'm sorry. I'm pretty disgusting here. Yup. I do sound just like *her*. No. I think I'm worse. So. From here on, no more complaining, whining, pissing, moaning, or anything like it. If I do, kick me. Better yet, stick me with your hiking pole. You can shove it right up my ass, where it belongs. Seriously, no more whining," I answered.

And I was serious. I meant it. I would be Polly Positive hence forth. No matter what happened, I would be nothing but cheerful. I could fall down, break a leg, split open my head, vomit, have diarrhea, whatever. I would find the good in all of these things. From here on out, I would be one big ray of sunshine. I would be toting nothing but good Karma. Looking back, I can't exactly say I lived up to being that inspirational, but I did stop bitching about the hills. Good thing. The trip would have been one big bitch-fest if I hadn't. Thanks Julie, for calling me out on my shit attitude. And for inviting me to join your adventure.

Continuing on after reaching that first summit, which when looking at our AT Guide really wasn't that impressive, we sat down on a couple of rocks to rest and hydrate. Sweat, sweat, sweat. That's what we were doing. Me, more than Julie because I had been too stupid to wear shorts and a t-shirt. It was at this point it might have been a good idea for me to put on my newly fashioned sports bra. I did not think of that. 2.6 miles into the trail, we came upon the Quarry Gap Shelter, which boasted a small stream in front of it. I do mean small. It was the size of a very little wading pool. You know, the three foot diameter type that is about six inches deep. Still, it wasn't stagnant, and we were able to filter water. This was my first lesson with the filter. It's actually very simple. There is a little gizmo about three inches long that screws onto the top of a plastic bag. First, you fill the plastic bag, then screw the gizmo in place, tip it upside down, and let it pour into any containers you might want to fill. Easy peasy. Having never tasted fresh, filtered spring water, I was pleasantly surprised at how refreshing it was. I guess I have never tasted water without some sort of chemical added to it. It is amazing.

I drenched my head and face with the water and cooled off. It was so hot there would be no problem with drying, and for the few minutes I was wet I felt really good. At this point I was very glad there were no mirrors around. I was sort of a hot mess. Literally, because I was sweating so profusely. Changing into a t-shirt, finally, I sat down, and realized I did not feel well. Of course I checked my pulse. Right. I wouldn't be missing an opportunity to fret about that. No problem. No skips. A bit of tachycardia but considering the climb, the heat, and my ability to put out sweat, that would be expected.

Julie suggested I eat something, so I choked down a protein bar. I was not the least bit hungry, which seemed odd considering what I had done so far today. I laid down in this very clean and beautiful, yes, beautiful shelter. To say it was immaculately maintained would be a massive understatement. It looked like an open front log cabin, divided into two sections. The floors had been painted dark green, and there was a broom and dustpan so that hikers could keep it clean. Hanging baskets of flowers adorned the outside, and there was a wooden swing, much like you would keep on your patio. There were no cushions, but still, it was sure a nice touch. The immediate ground was covered with inlaid rock, which was as near to pristine as one could hope to find in the middle of the woods. Yes. I would eat off that ground. I did not want to leave this place. Not today, anyhow.

We rested for about an hour, and when I saw Julie getting ready to put her pack back on, I panicked. Just a little.

"Jule, how far to the next shelter?"

"Oh, let me look. Uh...a little over seven miles. That's not too bad," she said.

Just shoot me now, I thought. No way did I have seven miles left in me. I was exhausted. Hopefully, if I rested for the rest of the day, got some sleep, ate and drank enough, I would be OK for tomorrow.

But, true to my new, rosy, sunshiny attitude, I meekly asked, "What if we just stayed here for tonight? It's so pretty......and there's water....and I am fucking wasted."

"Oh. Yeah, I guess we could. It's been pretty hot today, and we walked all that extra way trying to find the trail. I've heard about this shelter, and it's supposed to be the nicest one on the whole trail," answered Julie.

"Thanks, Jule....but I feel bad slowing you down."

"I got pretty tired at first, too. And didn't have much appetite. I think you need to take in more calories, and drink more water," she suggested.

"Yeah, you're probably right. I guess I underestimated the trail a little," I began.

"You'll be fine. You just need to get used to it," encouraged Julie.

With that, I laid down again for a while and had to admit that after more water and the protein bar, I was feeling better. I just didn't want to hike another seven miles that day, which was fine, because we decided to camp where we were.

"Let's put up the tent instead of sleeping inside the shelter. Sometimes it gets pretty crowded and smelly in them. People come in really late at night, and you could get stuck way in the back," explained Julie.

What did I know? If she suggested the tent, I was fine with

that. Well, let me correct that. I was fine until we put it up, and I actually saw how big it was. I know that the label read two-person tent. Looking at it I can understand how, with a little imagination, one could call it that. However, in reality, it should have been labeled a two-child tent. It would be fairly comfy for a couple of average sized nine year olds. We were not nine. Thankfully, we were thin.

Without stating the obvious, we both surveyed the tent and looked at each other.

"I could sleep in the shelter," I offered.

"Well, yeah, but I think we'll be OK," said Julie.

"Maybe we should sleep head to foot. That would give us a little more room. What do you think?" I suggested.

"I hadn't thought of that, but I think you're right. We have these side vents to open, too, so we get some air flow."

What the hell. We decided that we might as well try it tonight because if we got to a campground without a shelter, at least we would know it could be done. With our bedroom erected, our water bottles filled, my head freshly soaked with water, I was definitely relaxing. My tachycardia was gone. I didn't even need to pulse check for that one. I could just tell. Deciding to explore our evening's surroundings, I walked up to the outhouse, wonder-if all of the shelters had them. It stunk, as one would expect, but was in decent condition. I could deal with bad stinks. Being a nurse required it. One could not be a nurse if one could not overcome a bad stink without gagging. Or throwing up.

There was another hiker in the shelter when we arrived, and it appeared that he was not going anywhere that day, either. His gear was sprawled out, and he sat propped up against a side wall reading. I suppose if he had been on the trail for a while this was like coming to a five-star hotel, and if he wasn't too rushed on getting to Mt. Katahdin this would be the place for some R and R. Rest and reading. He was quiet and had not greeted us in any way. Maybe he was shy, just too tired, or not at all interested in us.

Whatever. No matter.

Several hours into our stay another hiker came along. He dropped his load and started to unpack his gear. It was obvious he would be spending the night. Within five minutes, he was stripped down to his boxer brief underwear. Yup. Right there in front of us he had taken off all of his clothes. Except for the boxer briefs.

"I don't know what your trail name is, but from now on as far as we're concerned, you're Boxer Brief," Julie said to him.

He told us his real trail name, which I did not write down, nor did Julie, so we have since forgotten. It wouldn't have mattered though, because he was absolutely Boxer Brief to us. Actually, he was quite a pleasant young man, about the age of our own kids. He sported a significant number of tattoos, told us he was a veteran, and then mumbled something about a little problem with a positive heroin test, adding that he did get an honorable discharge. We exchanged a little more pleasant conversation, and then I experienced the absolute pinnacle of my entire hiking trip.

Boxer Brief looked at me, and said, with total sincerity, "You must really hike a lot, because you have beautiful hiker legs!"

Oh. My. God. I cannot find words to express the ecstatic feeling those little words caused in me! Imagine! Sixty-one years old and this kid tells me I have great legs! Are you kidding?? Amazing! To be fair, I did have on black tights, and I suppose from a distance, I cut a decent shape. I keep saying that I look pretty good at forty yards out. But here he was, not more than ten feet away, telling me I have beautiful legs. I mean, he didn't tell Julie, he told me!! I have to admit, he did wear glasses, and perhaps his prescription had long ago expired. In any case, whatever his eyesight might be like, I was beyond thrilled with the complement.

"Thanks! You made my day!" I said.

"Ha! Made your day! He made this whole trip for you!" exclaimed Julie.

We did not make a campfire that evening, and the other guys in the shelter didn't suggest anything about one. Wise idea so far as I was concerned. It was hot, humid, sticky, and although the smell of burning wood would have been better than the smell of stinking people, I was still glad we didn't make even more heat. I ate my first freeze dried meal on the trail. Vegetable primavera and although I still wasn't very hungry, I have to admit it tasted good, and I felt much better with a full belly.

We spent the night facing head to foot in Julie's tiny tent enduring sauna conditions, me on my piece of shit worthless self-inflating mattress pad, and Julie happily on the one she blew up. I used the term "spent the night," because I did not sleep very much. Maybe I didn't sleep at all. I became adept at crawling in and out of the tiny flap because of course, given the inconvenience, I got up three times to pee. And I have to confess, I did not walk up to the outhouse. It was too far and too smelly. I peed in the bushes, not far from the tent. I know. Disgusting. Once again, Julie snored. I sort of hated her for being able to fall asleep so quickly and to remain in that wonderful land of slumber. Me? I held vigilance in the land of the wide-eyed, hearing the buzz of mosquitoes, with my hip bones resting heavily on the very hard, wooden floor under my crap mattress. Oh yes. I don't want to leave out mentioning the hot flashes. They came in between the pee trips. Nice. Fuck.

Chapter 8: Naked Bathing: Friday, July 8:

We got up shortly after sunrise. Although I didn't sleep much I suppose that the little dozing I was able to accomplish was worth something. I did feel a whole lot better than the night before. Julie broke out the teeny little camp stove, which is really just a cup type thing that boils water. We drank our coffee and tea, ate our cereal, filled up our water bottles and packed up camp. We noticed several other hikers had settled into the shelter during the night, and Boxer Brief was prancing around the grounds in his signature attire. Before we finished packing up our gear I did a very foolish, thoughtless thing, for which I am still ashamed. I have tried to repress this act, but it keeps poking through my memory movies like a bad commercial. I don't know what I was thinking. I like to attribute it to still not quite feeling like myself from the previous day's exertion, or maybe it was some sort of early dementia. Whatever prompted me to blurt this out, I can only say, I so very much regret it.

"Hey, Boxer Brief, do you want some alcohol for your hike? I've got a couple of those little bottles like they give you on the airplane. Peach schnapps, whiskey, and vodka. I'm trying to lighten my load here. I know they don't weigh much, but every ounce counts," I said conveying what I figured was a very generous offer.

"SANDY! WHAT ARE YOU DOING?" exclaimed Julie. I won't say she exactly yelled, but the volume of her voice definitely turned up a few notches.

"Oh….I was thinking we probably wouldn't really need it and figured I'd do better if my pack was a little lighter," I answered, meekly.

"Give me the God damned bottles. I'll carry them. What the fuck are you thinking?? We NEED them!"

Oh my. And Julie wasn't even much of a drinker. Boxer Brief quickly refused my kind offer, telling us he didn't drink. That made a certain amount of sense to me, having thought of his heroin incident. He was smart not to be using any controlled substances, if indeed he wasn't. Or, maybe Julie just scared the shit out of him when she sort of yelled.

"Jule, that's OK. I guess I can still carry them," I offered.

"Give them to me. I'll keep them. This way you won't be tempted to give them away again. Shit. We have so few amenities out here, and you're trying to take away our happy hour," said Julie.

"I guess I had a weak moment. Must be the heat, you know?"

I handed over the measly three little one ounce bottles. I should have just stuffed them back into my belly bag, but when she insisted on keeping them, I figured what the hell. The fact that she already had the heavier pack because of the tent, stove and water purification stuff was lost on me for a moment. Or, perhaps I am just sort of an ass. I did justify my handing over of the goods by telling myself that she was in better physical shape than I was and had a less arthritic back. Plus, she was younger. Two years is two years. Yeah. I repressed her neck issues here. Clearly, I really am an ass.

We quickly put the alcohol incident into perspective and joked about it a few times during the remainder of our hike. My choice of clothing for the day was much more prudent. Cell service was spotty, but when we were able to get it we checked the weather, and it looked like mid ninety temperatures for the rest of the week. Today I rolled up my pants, wrinkly skin be damned and wore the only t-shirt I brought. No hat was needed so I draped that from my waist. I soaked the bandanna I'd brought in the stream and tied that around my head. Not that anyone cared or cares, but I looked better with the bandanna than the hat. I suppose it would matter for pictures. No one likes to look like shit in their picture. Admittedly, having some good photos from this trip was important to me. Who knew if there would ever be another hike like this one?

We set forth onto the trail at about 8:30 AM, and I have to say,

I felt good. It was nice to have it a little cooler, and we trekked along at a pretty steady pace. The terrain was varied, with beautiful rhododendrons cascading along the narrow path, jungle type brush, steep areas of rock, and wider sections of just a plain old dirt path. There were several streams along our way which allowed us to re-fill water bottles and me to dunk my head. Having short hair for this venture is a very good idea. The shorter, the better. Hiking the AT is not so good for longhairs. Literally. I could not imagine having to brush out a big mane of tangles. I suppose dreadlocks would be another option, but they always just looked so heavy to me. How does one wash them? They must stink after a while.

Actually, I could have managed better with even shorter hair and had I planned on being out there for as long as Julie, would have chopped off what little I had left. There wasn't much thought of fashion, at least for me. Julie on the other hand, wore earrings. I didn't get that. Sure, I had my little studs filling my pierced ears, which I always wore because I was too lazy to change earrings unless there was some big occasion. In my life, there were not many of those.

Julie wore those dangly things. Plus, she kept her hat on. It was not one of those safari hats like mine, either. Uh uh. Like her brother, she sported a real cowboy hat. It looked both hot and heavy, but she said it was very comfortable. She even splatted on some kind of skin cream. It wasn't sunscreen, either. I'm not sure what she was using, but had to admit, she looked one shitload better than I did. I was happy with my green Camp Good Days and Special Times bandanna. Maybe she wanted to look better because she was going to be on the trail longer and didn't want to get some pathetic trail name, like Wrinkle Face, or Granny Pants. Whatever, she maintained some pride in her appearance. I did not.

True to my word, I did not complain about the hills, the heat, or the bugs. Actually, the bugs were only slightly bothersome. The organic essential oil deer and tick pasty stuff we purchased at

The Outfitter store back in Corning really seemed to be working. It didn't have any toxic chemicals and smelled good. We reapplied it every few hours because of our constant sweating. At least we weren't out in the open today, which was very good for us. It was so, so humid, and so, so hot. The woods afforded a bit of relief from the heat.

Today's hike was an amazing accomplishment for me. My back didn't hurt, my knees didn't ache, I wasn't doing pulse checks, and for the first time in a very long while I wasn't thinking about my age and what I might not be able to do. I thought only of getting myself and this pack on my back up the hills, over the streams, through the brush, and to the next shelter as indicated in our trail guide. There have been few times in my adult life when I have lived for "just in the moment" and I can actually recall when they were and what I was doing. The first bike trip from Buffalo to Gloucester, Massachusetts was one, my trip to Europe with John another, and our first charter boat sail into The Thousand Islands was a third. Maybe there have been more, but I can't readily recall them. Today, I would be adding to that list. I was in the moment.

I wasn't thinking about the home I'd left behind and the infinite number of daily activities that went along with living in our modern day world. I did not anticipate what would be waiting for me when I returned. I thought of my family, but only briefly. Mostly, I just looked for the next white blaze on a tree, marveled at the woods surrounding me, and felt blessed and fortunate to be out here trudging along, carrying everything needed for survival, at least for a few days, on my back.

I know. Julie had the tent, stove, and water stuff. But I could survive without those things. Dinner might leave something to be desired, and I would have to make it to a shelter since I had no tent. Some of the other hikers didn't bother filtering from the clear streams, so I could forego that as well. I was feeling competent, self-sufficient, and was mindless of my age. Yes. My buried spirit was emerging. I was beginning to think that maybe I needed more time out here.

Arriving at Birch Run Shelter in the mid afternoon we were dirty, sweaty, smelly, and refreshingly tired. This was a beautiful place, deep, deep in the woods. The shelter itself had eight bunks which are actually slabs of wood built into the walls. Maybe the proper term is rack. Whatever, they afford a place off the ground to place sleeping bags. There was a camping area next to this shelter and a stream about one hundred yards in front of it. This was the largest one we had encountered on the trail, and although it was by no means deep enough to swim in, there was a very fast, steady flow of water, and there were sections where it was about a foot deep.

Without any hesitation, without checking to see if anyone was presently in the shelter, we both stripped naked. Yes. Naked. Out came the tea sized towels we each carried, and we sponged off in the coldest, most refreshing water I have ever felt. It. Was. Magnificent! We rinsed our clothes, soaked our hair, and reveled in our new found cleanliness! Neither of us gave a thought to whether other hikers would see us naked at the stream. We did not care. I suppose I would compare it to giving birth. There you are. Spread eagled in the delivery stirrups. Nurses, doctors, family, housekeeping staff, all might be either in the room or meandering about. You so do not care. All sense of former modesty is delivered with the baby. And from my own experience and what I have seen over the years, it never does return with the same degree of intensity.

When I was ten years old I went to great lengths to be sure no one would see me naked in the ladies locker room at the Maple City Pool. Today? Shit. I would change in the parking lot without the slightest hesitation. You may regain some sense of decency, but the modesty you once coveted is no longer there. You may not be looking for opportunities to get naked, but if it happens you just say, "Who cares?" Because likely no one really does. Not at this age. The concern now is the possibility of scaring the onlooker.

It was like that for us at the stream. It wasn't that we were hoping to be seen. It's just that getting the dirt, caked on sweat, and horrid stink off us was our primary concern. Hey, we aren't twenty anymore. Or thirty, forty, or fifty. We're fast approaching that point in life where although you really don't care if someone sees you naked, there is a part of you that wants to spare them the experience. Stretch marks and cellulite, unlike wine and cheese, don't get better with age. But then, with proper marketing, perhaps those attributes could become the coveted traits women could strive to obtain. Whereas now the commercials tout creamy, youthful skin, with just a little spin, they could focus on a few creases and dimples. Maybe I should look into this concept.

Once we were as clean as we could hope to get and sufficiently cooled off, we dressed in our "camp clothes." Those are what hikers put on at the end of the day once they get to a shelter or pitch a tent. If opportunity presents, as it did today for us, they may rinse the clothes they hiked in all day. It's not like we carry much extra in the way of apparel, but most hikers seem to have at least one spare pair of socks, underwear, long sleeved shirt, some type of pants or shorts, and maybe some flip-flops. These are called camp clothes because often what you hike in all day is so wet and dirty, that continuing to wear them is just plain uncomfortable, and you really, really stink.

"Jule, how far did we go today," I asked, once we dressed and were unpacking our gear up at the shelter.

We staked out our "racks" for the night, so that as other hikers came in, they would know what was available.

"About 7.4 miles, according to the trail guide. And from the time it took us, that seems about right," answered Julie.

Can I say just exactly how impressed with myself I was at that news? Extremely impressed. Now that mileage may seem negligible to a seasoned hiker. But to me, after the rough start I'd had the day before and considering the preparation I had done, it was nothing short of a miracle. I felt good. I was hungry. I was relatively clean. I rocked it. Really. I owned this trail. OK. Maybe I am getting just a little carried away here. Actually, I am just pleased to say that I made it from the Quarry Gap Shelter to Birch Run, with no apparent mishaps. This was good. And I wasn't checking my pulse.

The only thing our shelter was missing was lawn furniture, or maybe a swing, like at the last shelter. That would have been a nice touch. Lacking that, I sat at the edge of the shelter opening, dangling my feet off, just feeling very contented and smug. Julie was rummaging through her things and getting our dinner items together. Thank God she intervened when I tried to give away our cocktails. Today, there would be a happy hour.

Shortly after our arrival, a couple who appeared to be toting really, really heavy packs, walked up to the picnic table at the front of the shelter and started unloading a whole lot of gear. We introduced ourselves, and they did the same. We still didn't have official trail names, so went by just our first names. Slosh and Scavenger however, were thru-hikers, so they had long ago acquired their official monikers. They appeared to be in their thirties, both had British accents, and stunk. Badly. They, or rather Slosh, the guy, started meal preparations. We watched in amazement at what he was pulling from his pack. Tomatoes, onions, peppers, seasonings, pans, bowls, a small stove that could actually do more than boil water, and pasta. It smelled so good! Our own fare would be a package of freeze dried spaghetti, which contained meat. I was stressing a little about the fact I would be eating part of a cow. But these were desperate times. I was hungry. I mean, really, really hungry. I would have to suffer the guilt, but was already rationalizing this sin.

However, it appeared that the stinky British couple's dinner was vegetarian. Maybe they would offer to share. I would look longingly at the picnic table and engage them in conversation, although I knew that feeding us was not realistic, or practical. It was tough enough carrying your own food without lugging along enough for a potluck. Still, I continued to hope for a miracle.

"Where are you guys from?" I asked.

"England," answered Scavenger, the woman.

"Oh. What brought you to the states? Did you come planning to hike?" I continued with my interrogation and my ever increasing hope of a dinner invitation. Julie continued sorting and organizing her gear.

"Actually, yes. We got visas so we need to finish by October 5th. We both quit our jobs to do this," Scavenger continued.

"Wow! So, you're thru-hikers. When did you start? We're just doing a section. Actually, I'm only here for about a week. Julie will be staying til the middle of August," I continued.

"And I have to ask you, how did you get your trail names?"

"Well, in the beginning, I was drinking a bit and had quite a few days where I was pretty well sloshed. I've stopped that and lost about fifty pounds. I was pretty fat when we started. Scavenger here is always scrounging food off people, so that's where her name comes from," he explained, in his very British accent.

"We haven't been out here very long yet, so we still don't have names. You said you quit your jobs back home. What did you do?" I asked.

I was curious. It seemed like a pretty big deal to pull up roots, fly across the ocean, and hike across a foreign country. Here I thought we were awesome for driving a couple of hours south and hitting the trail.

"Slosh is actually a chef. He does all of the cooking on this hike, too. I worked in hospitality, but it was definitely time to make some changes. We came up with this hiking idea, and then we'll figure out what to do when we get back home," explained Scavenger, while picking away at the food scraps Slosh was casting off.

Our conversation continued, and we learned they were married and had been for over ten years. We discussed the political scene, because BREXIT just happened, and we were dealing with our own catastrophe here with the presidential campaign, not realizing at the time how much worse things would be getting for both of our countries.

Once Slosh finished with the meal preparation, more utensils were pulled out of his pack, and dining began in earnest. For them. Not us. Clearly potluck was not going to be happening this afternoon. As they ate, they told us they planned on hiking another six miles before bedtime. That was impressive. I thought we were amazing with our 7.4. At this point, six miles would have been a full day's hike for me. As they finished, we watched in awe as they washed off their dishes, packed up the leftovers, and stuffed everything back into his pack. I asked if I could pick it up. Please note that I said *his* pack. It just looked so very heavy, and I couldn't imagine carrying all of the kitchen tools that I had seen.

The stuff was not being divided equally as it was being shoved back in. I got to thinking just how nice it would be if we had a big strong boy or a man with us. He could be our Sherpa. It sure would make this backpacking thing a lot easier. If he could cook, that would be an extra bonus. We could eat like these British folks, and scrap the freeze-dried stuff. It wasn't that freeze dried was bad. I liked it fine. When I cracked open a package back home just to give my taste buds a test drive with it, my husband wanted to know why we didn't just eat it every night. He loved it. John is not exactly a foodie. He has been known to put relish in an omelet and jelly in his coffee, so I don't always take his recommendations seriously.

"Sure, but really, it isn't that heavy," said Slosh.

Miraculously I managed to lift the albatross off the ground, but just barely. Actually strap it on and carry it? No way. The thing weighed seventy-five pounds, if it weighed an ounce. Unbelievable. No wonder they smelled so bad. He must break out into a sweat just strapping it in place.

"Jule, do you think anyone else will come? Wouldn't it be great to have the whole shelter to ourselves and not have to smell any bad stinks?"

"That would be great, but don't plan on it. People keep rolling in even after dark. I haven't been alone at night since I started. Actually, when I'm by myself I always hope somebody else shows up. I like knowing I'm not out here alone," she said.

"Yeah, if I was by myself, I'd feel the same way. It's kind of unnerving in the woods at night."

It was getting on toward time for happy hour. I retrieved our now very coveted alcohol stash, and we had ourselves a toast. As we chatted about our day, hikers started trickling in. First, came a very young man, maybe early twenties. Getting him to talk took some effort. We weren't sure if he was just shy, or maybe a little nervous talking with women old enough to be grandmothers. We learned his name was Lt. Dan, taken from the character in the *Forest Gump* movie. I have to say, he did kind of look like the guy. Questioning him didn't provide much information other than his actual age, which was twenty-three, and the fact he was hiking by himself because the friend he started out with met a girl and left the trail to be with her.

Next, an even younger lone guy limped in. A baby! Really! I don't even think he shaved yet.

"Hi, welcome! Hey, you have quite a limp there. Are you OK?" I greeted him.

"Hi. Actually, I've had a pretty long day. I've hiked about twenty-three miles, and my knee is killing me. I hope I haven't done something really bad to it."

He'd come to the right shelter. Here were two nurses, eager to share their medical opinions and motherly advice. His name was Rook, and he was only nineteen. These guys were both thru-hikers. Impressive at such a young age. Julie and I sure couldn't have done this when we were that age. We had enough trouble getting our homework done in college and spending every spare moment we could with our boyfriends (later husbands, and even later, ex-husbands). We would have been so very much better off hiking.

"So, what is it you guys are thinking you want to do when you get off the trail? I mean with the rest of your lives. College? Work? What do you like to do? Have you given any thought to student loans? What do your families think about your hiking?"

Yes. I really did ask these poor kids all of those questions. Having very recently retired from my job as a school counselor with a vocational high school, I couldn't seem to resist providing them with what I believed to be excellent career counseling. It is what I had done for over twenty-five years. It was what I knew. It definitely was not what was needed by these young men on this hike. However, they were polite, and they answered my questions, at least to the best of their nineteen and twenty-three year old abilities.

Lt. Dan was floundering and didn't know what he wanted to do. He'd had some contracting experience and was taking this time to sort things out with his life. Rook had started college, but things didn't quite work out as he intended, so he was also taking the time to hike, think, and figure out what to do next.

I suggested going to college or trade school to the both of them. Julie suggested Rook take a week off to rest his injured knee and get himself some anti-inflammatory medication, like Ibuprofen. These boys were so very nice to us. I suspect they thought of us as mothers or grandmothers. They even made the campfire, and it was from them we learned Purell makes excellent lighter fluid. Who would have thought? I suppose it was a trade-off. Health and career information for trail tips. We all shared what we knew. We all win.

Before the health and career counseling session and the campfire, yet another hiker ambled into Birch Run. I had one hell of a time extracting any information from her, but my tenacity paid off, and I eventually learned that she was a forty-two year old woman from Boston who had been on the trail by herself for three months. She confessed it was a life-long dream to hike the entire twenty-one hundred miles, but was only able to commit three months, so knew she would only get about half way. Tomorrow was to be her final day on the trail, so she was kind of mourning the end of her dream. She would return to the "real world" and the city. Even though I had only been out here for a couple of days, I could completely understand why those who spent months here in the woods might find transitioning back to "regular civilization" difficult and not all that enticing.

Here, there were so few decisions to be made. Meals consisted of whatever could be carried in your backpack. Clothing was not necessarily changed every day, and even if it was, there was likely only one other item to replace it. Although cell service was available from time to time, it wasn't like hikers were staring at their phones, because they were too busy watching the ground so they wouldn't trip and fall, or step on an unsuspecting rattlesnake.

The choices of what to do in the evening were limited because you were likely too exhausted to do much other than filter water, prepare dinner, spread out your sleeping area, and if wood and Purell were available, make a fire. I really, really liked the simplification of life out here. I could understand why hikers were sometimes drawn back to the trail, or onto other challenges, like the Pacific Coast Trail. That was way out of my league, but I could see myself looking for other hikes once this adventure ended. Already, I could see myself returning to the AT, another section, at another time, perhaps in another state.

I did not get the trail name of the Boston woman. Since she was not forthcoming with information sharing and unless I wanted to get even more assertive with my questions than I already was, I'd best just concentrate on my career counseling with the boys. She was pleasant enough, just a little odd. My go-to description for people like that is, "just a little off center mark." I did learn that she was somehow involved with clergy, although I don't know if she was actually a minister. I do know she wasn't a nun.

Julie didn't participate in the line of questioning. She isn't as pushy as I so often can be. She was, however, very helpful to the young man who complained of knee pain. She seemed to know specifically the name of the tendon that was likely causing his problems. We tag teamed on his plan of care. She pushed for rest and Ibuprofen; I encouraged the continuing education.

Rounding out our little party here at Birch Run was a young couple from Georgia. We learned they were married, and he was a substance abuse counselor considering going back to school to become a teacher. His wife was a special education teacher. I don't recall the story regarding their joblessness, but they were thru-hikers, so neither of them were working at the time.

Listening to them tell of their adventures made me regret some of the shitty choices I'd made in my younger years. I mentioned this to Julie and she agreed. I mean, hey, we could have been kick-ass hikers! We did well enough running the marathons, with cheap shoes, poor training, generally being dehydrated, eating junk food, and not stretching. We've often talked about what we could have accomplished if we knew what we were doing and if we hadn't gotten married that first time so very, very young. Very young, very naive, and very short sighted is what we were. And yeah, very stupid.

However, since no one has figured out how to turn back the clock, the best thing to do is not continue to make the same mistakes. Maybe we can no longer run a marathon in less than four hours, but we sure as hell can climb these freaking hills! We've started a new decade, and we are going to rock it. Well, at least we are going to shake it up some.

I finally slept decently, primarily because Julie suggested I try and blow some more air into the piece-of-shit-self-inflating mattress pad. It worked. The thing gained an inch in thickness. Maybe that doesn't seem like much, but being an inch *off* the hard ground is a vast improvement over being *on* the ground. Or the wooden rack, which is just as hard as ground.

When I say I slept decently, I might clarify just a little. I slept decently for me, but still like shit. Once again, the inconvenience of bathroom facilities prompted me to get up three times during the night. I heard the other people in the shelter snoring, and that not only kept me awake for awhile, but ticked me off, because it meant other people were sleeping. And, I. Was. Not. I also was awake for the additional two hikers who came in shortly before midnight. They were gone right after sun-up, so I can't tell you anything about them or what their trail names were. Obviously, they are pretty hardcore hikers if they are on the trail for that length of time in a day. Julie told me she'd had one sixteen hour day, which impressed the hell out of me. I guess I am just a princess hiker, because I think six hours is very excellent.

Laying in my rack on that 8th of July, nestled deep in the woods of Pennsylvania, I thought about my father. It would have been his ninety-sixth birthday. Although he never expressed interest in camping, saying that he had slept in enough tents during his army time, I think he would have gotten a kick out of what I was doing. Of course, he wouldn't admit it, though. He grew cantankerous in his later years, but during my growing up time, always encouraged me, seeming to have way more faith in my abilities than I ever did. I chuckled at the thought of what he likely would have said about the hike.

"You know, if it were me, I'd save my energy and stay in one of those nice motels, one with a pool." And then he would add, "You always do things the hard way."

He would have been right on both counts. Yes. He would have stayed in the motel, and I did sometimes seem to make my life more difficult than it needed to be.

Chapter 9: Splat: Saturday, July 9

Getting up before Julie, I made myself useful and retrieved our food bag from the steep iron pole from which it hung. There are such poles at some of the campgrounds and shelters on the trail to keep the bears away from sleeping hikers and also away from their food. Sometimes there are heavy iron boxes. When there are no such boxes or poles available, hikers just throw a rope over a high tree branch and haul the food up there for safe keeping. There are special bags that the hiker's food is sealed in each night, which of course are expensive. Actually, all hiking gear is expensive. I guess I would compare the stuff to boating supplies, whereby if it is marked *nautical quality*, regardless of what the product might be, it is also of *nautical pricing*, which is expensive. It is amazzing the type of products that can carry the term *nautical quality*.

Several years ago my husband bought some non-stick shelf liner paper from a well known boating store. He paid ten dollars for the roll, because sure enough, it was of nautical quality. Really? How does that apply to shelf liner? I mean, the boat isn't going to take on water if the shelves are lined with regular stuff. I'm not complaining here because his shelf-paper purchase was actually a favor to me. In all the years I've know the man, he has not exactly taken interest in the condition of our shelves, be them on the boat or in the house. However, I found the same roll of non-stick shelf liner at The Dollar Store. No, it didn't say *nautical quality* on the package, but the contents were identical. And I paid one dollar for the roll, not ten.

I was having a little trouble with the heavy, cumbersome pole used to free the hanging food bag, and lucky for me, Rook with the bad knee came along and retrieved it for me. He was limping and decided that he would indeed be getting off the trail, for at least a couple of days, and would be making arrangements for his father to pick him up. Meanwhile, Lt. Dan was also stirring. He packed up his gear and lit a joint. Hmm. Maybe we should have thought of that. He tried to be discreet about it, but if you grew up in the seventies, you knew the smell of pot. There is no mistaking it for something else.

We wished him well, packed up our own belongings, drank our tea/coffee, ate our cereal, lamented that we didn't have our own stash of pot, and then Julie stubbed her toe. I mean, she really stubbed it.

"Shit, fuck, damn, I think I broke my toe!" exclaimed Julie.

"Oh no, let me see! Can you move it at all?" I asked, stupidly.

Of course she couldn't move it. She's a nurse. The fact that she couldn't move it is what made her think she broke it in the first place.

"I'll just tape it to the next toe and hope for the best. I think I can walk OK with it. We won't be going fast," she said.

That was an understatement. With me along there was absolutely no possibility of walking fast. We hit the trail by eight, and Julie did seem able to manage alright. She said it was actually feeling a little better, and maybe she didn't break it after all. It would be a long, long day, at least for me. Our goal was to go ten miles and end at a place called Pine Grove Furnace, which is just past the halfway point of the trail. There was supposed to be a hostel we could stay at and also a small snack shop where we could get dinner. The place was known for selling half gallon containers of ice cream to thru-hikers who were just passing the halfway mark. Tradition had it that hikers would wolf down the entire container and then likely get sick, because it had been so long since they consumed food that rich. Interesting.

One thing about hiking the trail is that it provides a great appreciation for real food. I mean, like fruits and veggies, fresh bread and cheese, basically anything not processed, freeze dried, or spiked full of preservatives. My very short stint on the trail put me in touch with that on the first morning, when I was not able to add half and half to my tea, or pour freshly squeezed orange juice. I didn't so much mind eating out of the very lightweight metal dog food dish. That was fine. Hey, dog food might have actually been a step up from some of the trail food.

Looking back on my trail time, I would have to say that today's hike was the best. Julie spent much more time out there, and although I know she will remember this section pretty well, she likely has another "best." I liked today because of the varied terrain, the fact that although the temperature still climbed into the nineties, it didn't seem quite as humid. There were rolling hills and a few steep trails, although there were mostly switchbacks when it came to climbing. There was some of the thick, jungle type brush, but also some very wide sections where a car could have been driven comfortably through. The streams we encountered had plenty of water, so my head splashing ritual continued. I was now taking my t-shirt off whenever we came to a stream, dunking it into the icy cold water, ringing it out, and putting it back on. I did not care if other hikers saw me, although I did try to be discreet.

Remember that old Jeff Foxworthy comedy routine when he talked about seeing his grandmother naked? And it scared him so much? According to the comedy routine, it scarred him for life. The image was embedded in his brain like a footprint in concrete. Well, I certainly didn't want to frighten some young guy like that. Although for the girls who might see me, I could serve as the icon of why one should protect their skin from the ultraviolet rays of the sun. These horrific scenes never did come to fruition, which was probably for the best.

Since this was early into our week and actually only my third day on the trail, and because I had not prepared adequately with hikes longer than three miles, I started getting pretty tired at about the eight mile mark. At this point I was confident I would be OK, because I knew that our stopping point was just two more miles up the trail. I was feeling the hills more now, and sometimes I would count my steps, just to pass the time. Conversation just seemed like too much effort. At least it did for me, and from Julie's lack of introducing topics to discuss, it appeared to be that way for her as well.

Seeing the sign marking the distance to Pine Grove Furnace was epic. I was going to make it. I would have trekked a good ten miles today on the AT. We even passed the halfway point, where of course we had to stop for a photo op. If we were thrilled to be standing at the sign that read, Springer Mountain, Georgia, eleven hundred miles: Mt Katahdin, Maine, eleven hundred miles, imagine what the actual thru-hikers felt! Either they were energized and excited to know they had made it halfway, or they were totally exhausted and discouraged to think that they were now facing the really tough section with the rocks of Pennsylvania and the mountains of New England.

Posting the picture of me standing under this sign on Facebook got some great comments. Those who don't know me very well thought I had hiked the entire eleven hundred miles. It was with great hesitancy that I admitted to not yet having gone twenty miles. But I did clarify. I didn't really want to do that, but I'm not a total ass. I am pretty honest most of the time.

If you have ever gone downhill skiing and enjoyed the thrill of flying down a steep slope, swooshing from side to side as the blades of your skis dig into the snow and your hips sway effortlessly, then you understand that feeling of total abandon. Or like me, you have gone downhill skiing, snow plowing painfully slow, crisscrossing the slope so there is never too much speed built up. Your hips stiffly shift like a hinge that needs oil; you enjoy the fresh air but just don't abandon anything.

Either way you experience a challenge, and if you are really having a good time out there, don't always recognize feelings of fatigue. *Just one more run* is the mantra that goes through your head. What should be running in your head is the mantra, *body is tired, time to rest*. It is usually at the end of a day spent skiing that you start to fall. You get careless. You are tired.

When out on the trail, with a destination in mind, generally a necessary one, it's important to find a place to pitch your tent where there is water, flat ground, and a high place to store food and wrappers so the wild critters don't creep into your tent. With you still inside. Wrapped up in your sleeping bag. Hiking all day burns a lot of calories, expends a great deal of energy, and makes you tired. Like skiing, it's good to know when to stop and not try to hike what might be an absurd number of miles. When first beginning, without adequate training and practice, don't try for a twenty mile day. Or fifteen. Or even ten if the terrain is particularly mountainous.

Our goal of ten miles for today seemed realistic and attainable for us. I mean, I had practiced some, albeit not adequately. At least I could swim a long way. I now realized that didn't translate very effectively to carrying twenty-five pounds on my back and walking up a mountain. But still, at least I was being physically active, even if it wasn't especially useful toward hiking. Our mileage today was really progressing finely. We rested often, drank adequately, consumed what seemed to be enough calories.

But, like skiing, sometimes that fatigue thing just sort of sneaks up on you. On the trail, you may find yourself stumbling. Where earlier in the day your footing was confident and sure, now it's clumsy. This is when a longer rest would be in order. This is when I was so intent on getting to the end of our hike that I got careless. I was tired. The damned pack was heavy. I ached. And then, suddenly, my foot rolled a stone, and I splatted. I do mean, I really, really splatted. Shit.

"Fuck!" I exclaimed, as I went down hard on the rocks, with my right knee and elbow taking most of the impact.

It was an almost surreal feeling as I recall, because if I hadn't had the pack on, I likely could have caught myself and regained my footing. But the pack had a mind and life of it's own, and that baby took me down like a tackled football player. Once my foot rolled over on that rock, there was no getting my balance back. Can I just say, this really, really hurt. My immediate fear, before I took a minute to assess my injury, to do my personal triage, was that I had broken something. Maybe my elbow, maybe my knee. At least I hadn't whacked my head.

"Oh my God, are you OK? Don't get up. Just stay down. Take a few deep breaths," instructed Julie.

I suppose the fact we were both nurses was good. At least we knew the basics of what to do in case something like this happened. She helped me to a sitting position, and we checked me out.

"I think I'm OK. I just can't believe I've fucking fallen," I said.

When I get hurt, or angry, or frustrated, as mentioned earlier, I swear a lot. Fuck seems to be my go-to word. It ain't pretty but I always feel better after I've said a few of them. I suppose some people say Hail Marys. That would certainly be classier. I know the prayer well since I was raised Catholic, and at confession that was the usual assignment. I said a lot of Hail Marys for contrition in my day. But no. I couldn't recite a prayer. I had to let loose with the F bombs.

"Shit, I can't believe I did this. I was finally doing better. You know, carrying the pack on the hills and all."

"We're just tired. You rolled that stone, and your pack took you down. It's easy to do."

After literally shaking off the dust because it was a rocky dirt road that had taken me down so abruptly, I stood up. Assessing the damage, I found my right elbow to be gashed and bleeding, but it didn't appear deep enough to need stitches. My main concern was my right knee, which had really taken most of the force of one hundred twenty-five pound me and twenty-five pound pack. It was pretty tender, although I was able to walk alright.

"I'm OK. Really. Pretty lucky, I guess. I mean, I could have broken something. Must be I've got good bones!" I announced stoically.

"Jule, I think I know what my trail name should be. Splat."

She didn't argue. I sort of wish she had. I know that I can be self deprecating, but sometimes you do want people to denounce your self deprecations. When she didn't I felt a little bad, because I was hoping for a much cooler trail name. However, at this point, Splat did seem very appropriate. Julie helped me get my pack back on, and we continued to the Pine Grove Furnace General Store, which according to the trail guide was about a mile.

It was one very long mile. My knee throbbed, and my elbow stung, but the further we walked, the more certain I became that I would be fine, and this splat would go down as a minor blip on our hiking radar screen. Mostly, I was thinking just how lucky I was not to have broken any bones.

"Sandy, there's a hostel right by the general store. I think it would be cool to stay right there tonight. It's supposed to be pretty decent."

After one night in a mini-tent sleeping on a pad with the depth of a postage stamp and one night on a wooden rack in an open front shelter, anything under a roof with a running water spigot and mattress would seem like The Plaza. Hey, at this point I would have welcomed a chamber pot. That hostel sounded great to me. John and I stayed in one a few years ago in Cape Vincent which is at the mouth of the St. Lawrence River. It was actually part of the lighthouse and as I recall, was quaint, clean, and cozy. Yes. The hostel, a hot shower, dinner from the general store, and a real bunk sounded very excellent.

Except, when we reached the hostel, which was a very elegant old mansion, there was just this minor little problem with accommodations. There weren't any. The thing was closed. There was a big, fat, disgusting, closed sign chained across the driveway. Nice. Looking at each other, we simultaneously said, "Shit."

"Sandy, I think we should call for a ride and get back to your car. As long as we have it here, we can go to a motel for the night, get back on the trail tomorrow. I've got some phone numbers. That's what Bruce and I did when he left. People make a lot of money transporting hikers to towns and all. And we didn't have to wait long for the pick up."

Well, it was tough to argue with that one. A hot shower and soft bed sounded really good to me. Plus, I could get some ice for my knee. If I kept using ice tonight, maybe I could do some damage control with my knee and elbow. We could eat out. We could drink wine. A full glass of wine. Yes. Good plan.

Reaching that general store was a milestone for me. No, I still hadn't racked up twenty-five miles on the trail, but I had been out here for a couple of days. I knew I could carry my pack. I filtered water like a pro. I was dirty, sweaty, and I stunk. Yup, I was really an AT hiker now. The general store had a decent restroom, and I was able to clean up my elbow and sponge off some of the dirt. I got some ice for my knee, and we sat down to enjoy our ice cream. The place was busy, mostly populated with hikers, but there was a group of motorcycle people sitting next to us. They were roughly our age and appeared to be having a great time.

We struck up a conversation asking if they would take our picture. Of course they obliged as anyone with a phone these days is happy to do. I don't recall any of their names, but I believe there were four couples. They told us where they were from, and one couple actually lived about an hour away from Corning. They asked us about our hike and appeared to be extremely impressed with our adventure. They were particularly impressed with Julie's plan to spend most of the summer hiking by herself. I think that the women found this especially hard to imagine. They thought of themselves as pretty tough because they rode on the back of a motorcycle. I might add, these were not small cycles. They were big, wide, and totally loaded with amenities. These were the Cadillacs of motorcycles. Riding one of these babies would not be uncomfortable in any way. These women were not going to be getting hot and sweaty on a hiking trail. They were well coiffed. Lots of makeup, lots of jewelry, and pricey clothes.

Although all four ladies expressed a great deal of interest in both our ages and our intentions, it was the men who were really intrigued. They thought we were celebrities. Really. They did. They thought that we were incognito famous people and kept asking us what our real names were, what we really did, and promising not to tell anyone. This was a very interesting concept for the both of us, and we were totally enjoying it. More footage for our mental movie to play at the *home* when our times came.

Following our interlude with the bikers, Julie looked through her list of numbers and made several phone calls. Finally connecting with a woman, we were told that she could pick us up within the hour. Great. That hot shower was getting closer. After our motorcycle fan club departed and we'd finished our ice cream, we walked around the vicinity. Not having the packs on made us feel so light, so agile. Even with my aching knee and hip, I felt the spring come back into my slightly gimpy step.

I don't believe I mentioned injuring my hip before. That's because my knee and elbow hurt so much. They outranked my hip in pain intensity. Now that I'd iced my knee, cleaned up my elbow, and sat for a few minutes, the hip pangs kicked in. Checking my hip, I saw the beginnings of a bruise forming. Nice. I should ice that, too. Just to keep the swelling down. Hopefully it wasn't cracked.

True to her word, our ride showed up within the hour. All I can say is, "Oh. My."

This was really going to be interesting. The woman appeared to be about sixty, a little frumpy, and slightly unkempt. Suffice it to say, as bad as we looked, we were visions of beauty next to this old girl. Our ride back to Lucy was going to be in a rusty pickup, where we would be sitting three in the front seat. I don't know if this is legal in Pennsylvania, but this old girl didn't seem to be giving it a thought. I didn't write her name down at the time, nor did Julie, so of course don't remember what it was. For convenience sake, I'll refer to her as Ida. No offense intended toward any Idas' out there.

Ida was friendly enough. She jammed our packs into the back of the pickup, where the tailgate remained open, because she announced it didn't work but assured us the packs would be fine. One could only hope. There was only one seat belt for the entire front seat, and Ida used it. For herself. No problem. What were the chances of an accident? Although she drove fast. Very, very fast down winding, narrow roads. Shortly after leaving the Pine Grove General Store, Ida's phone rang. It was a flip phone. Clearly there was no bluetooth in this rig. Bluetooth had not been invented when this truck was born. She answered it.

"Hello. Yup. I've picked up a couple of hikers. Takin' em back to Caledonia Park to their car. Yup. Couple of ladies. I'll be home shortly," said Ida.

"WHAT? You're doing what? You can't do that! You need to get back to that hospital, and wait for a ride! Yes! I'll be there! Soon as I can! Did you hear me? You get right back to that hospital and wait!" demanded Ida, now visibly upset and going a little faster, if that was even possible.

To say that Julie and I were now fearing for our lives would be an understatement. Hey. Put us back on the trail. Stick a rattlesnake and a couple of bears in our path. That would likely be one shitload safer than being stuck in the front seat of this rust bucket with this wack-a-doodle. I started to pray. Yes. Me. I said a Hail Mary. No fucks here. Just real, genuine, sincere praying was going on. I don't know what Julie was doing, but I suspect she had her own go-to-prayer.

"Uh, are you sure you're OK giving us a ride? I mean we could find another one, if you have something to do," I said

"Oh no. This is no problem. B'sides, I can use the money. That was just my husband. Dwayne. He's older n'me, and his health isn't very good. He's been in the hospital because he stopped takin' his pills. Can you believe that? He's on all kinds of medications, and he just one day up and stopped takin'em. Said he didn't need em anymore and would be fine without em. Well, his blood pressure shot through the roof, he passed out, and I had to call an ambulance. They've had him there a week gettin' his pills back on track," explained Ida

"You know how men can be. And he calls here and tells me they've discharged him, and he's walkin' home. Can you believe that? We live miles from the hospital. If he doesn't go back, I'll just have to drive along til I find him and pick him up," continued Ida.

"Really, it's no problem if you need to drop us off. I have more numbers I can call. We can get another ride," said Julie, clearly hoping Ida would pull over and let us out, where we could safely hitchhike.

"Naw, that's OK. It's no problem. Not that far to the park, then I'll just pick the old boy up. Say, if you're lookin' for a place to stay tonight, our church runs a youth hostel. Lots a' hikers stay there. I'm the minister. In fact, I was just workin' on my sermon when I got your call. We only charge twenty dollars for the night. You'd have a hot shower and a bed. I can take you right there, if you'd like,"offered Ida.

I knew I sure as hell didn't want to stay there, and when Julie poked me in the ribs, which was easily done in the cramped front seat of Ida's small pickup truck, I quickly responded.

"Thanks so much, but we need to get to a store for some groceries and other supplies. We'll just go to town and check into a motel. We need to do some laundry, too," I said.

"We got a washer an' all right at the hostel, and the store isn't far. I could drive you there," offered Ida.

Now I was getting worried. I assume Julie was as well. Maybe she wasn't going to let us out. She sure was pushing her hostel on us. Again we declined, and this time, she didn't pursue the issue.

"You girls know anything about old men and counselin'?

Dwayne's almost eighty, and he's just miserable to live with. Sometimes, I don't know how I do it. Even with the Lord an all, givin' me guidance n' strength, it's just so hard some days. He's stubborn, mean, and won't take care of himself. I keep wishin' he'd go talk to a counselor. Maybe the hospital'll make him. Do you think they would?"

Well, this *was* my area of expertise. Not that I am much of an expert on anything, but I did spend over twenty-five years working in the schools as a counselor. No, there were no old men on my caseload, but with a little imagination, I suppose I could stretch and count the elderly pedophile who was the father of one of my students. I spoke with him several times on the phone regarding his daughter, because he wanted me to tell her to just move back home and quit making trouble. Those were tough calls for me because basically, I just wanted to choke the creep.

But then, people are people. We all want basically the same thing; we just have our different methods of pursuing those basics. Given what Ida had just shared about Dwayne, the chances of him ever talking to any kind of counselor, therapist, social worker, psychologist, etc. were slim to none. I would wager my retirement income on none. However, I didn't want to sound too discouraging, and in all fairness, I had not met Dwayne. Julie remained silent. Apparently, she was deferring to me on this one. Thanks, bitch.

"Well, it's tough to make someone go to a counselor if they don't really want to talk about their problems. Have you mentioned this idea to Dwayne?"

"Oh Lord, yes. All the time. He just tells me he ain't talkin' to no shrink. And he keeps right on bein' miserable. If I wasn't a Godly woman, I would've left him a long time ago. I just can't do that now, because he's so old. You know how it is. I don't know what would happen to him. He might kill himself. So, I just keep prayin' n' tryin' to live with the miserable old goat. We all have our crosses to bear," answered Ida.

Miraculously, we reached Lucy in the park. Paying Ida twenty dollars each, which I think is a very good deal for her, and a small price for us to pay to get away, we unloaded from the pickup and re-loaded into Lucy. Ida offered to come pick us up in the morning and drive us back to the trail. We very politely, and quickly, declined her generous offer. Generous, right. Another easy forty bucks for her plus some time away from Dwayne. Come to think of it, it was Dwayne who she offered as our chauffeur. She mentioned having to preach in church, so Dwayne could come and drive us. We simultaneously shuddered at the thought. Ewwww. Squashed three in the front seat with Dwayne?? No. Not ever. And, no more Ida.

Happily resting in Lucy, we pulled out of the park and headed for Chambersburg, where we found a Clarion Inn and checked in. This would be so excellent. We could eat at the Ruby Tuesdays next door, do our laundry, catch up on our Facebook pages, take hot showers, and best of all, sleep off the ground. Except. You know how sometimes things never work out exactly the way they're planned? We had a few problems.

Checking in, we could see that the front desk clerk was extremely frazzled. He was obviously not having a good day. And his evening didn't appear to be looking up, either. Folks were giving him a really tough time. I overheard some of the conversation. I mean, how could I help it? I was standing three feet away, waiting my turn to check in. Julie was next to me, and we patiently stood as the woman rattled off one complaint after another, in a very righteous tone. It's like she had paid thousands of dollars for the night. I mean, really. It was The Clarion for God's sake, not The Ritz. Or The Carlton. Or, even The Hilton.

"And the air conditioner wouldn't work on the high setting, the hot water was slow to start, there was no coffee packet for the coffee machine, the volume of the TV wouldn't go loud enough so that we could hear properly, and there was a wrinkle in the pillowcase."

OK. So I made up the pillowcase part. But you get my point. Either this place, which looked like it was maintained well enough was a fleabag in disguise or this woman was one demanding bitch.

The kinda meek clerk smiled and very politely told her that he would check into all of her issues (complaints). At that, her voice register and the volume went up a few notches. She began her litany of demands for if not a full refund, at least some recognition for her inconvenience. The matter was settled with an apology and a partial refund, which I wasn't fully comprehending, but then I was tired. Julie was tired. We'd had a long day on the trail. I'd splatted. My elbow stung, my hip and knee ached, we'd ridden with crazy Ida, listened to her stories of miserable Dwayne, and we were done. Any room with any bed and mattress would be fine with us.

"Rough day?" I said to the clerk when it was our turn.

Visibly a little shaken and not up to his best game, he just smiled slightly and replied, "Oh, no problem. It's fine. What can I help you ladies with?"

We checked in, took our room keys, grabbed a cart for our gear, and headed for tonight's shelter. Interesting, when we're on the trail we carry everything on our back. When we get to town we need a cart to move our belongings. What is wrong with this picture? Settling into our room, which incidentally, was very nice, we noticed the air conditioning, hot water, and TV were functioning just fine. Gathering up our dirty clothes, we headed to the laundry room. Likely this would be the only chance for the next week to actually use machines and not stream water to clean our clothes.

Showered, clad in the extra clothes I kept in my gym bag, which I shared with Julie, we walked to the adjoining Ruby Tuesdays for dinner. And wine. Full glasses of wine, not the tiny little one ounce shots of vodka that we had for the trail. I also took this opportunity to hold ice on my bruised and very sore knee. I couldn't do the same for my hip unless I pulled my pants down.

Somehow, that just didn't seem like a good idea while we were eating. In a public place. I shuddered at the thought.

It was on our way to the laundry room where we planned to move our freshly washed clothes to the dryer before returning to our room, that I discovered I didn't have my room key.

"Jule, I must have forgotten the room key. Do you have yours?"

"Uh, no. I never got one. He gave you both, remember?"

"Yeah, guess he did. Except I don't have either one. Guess we need to go back to the desk. Wonder if the same guy'll be there?" I asked.

"Hi. What's your first name? Shawan? That's a nice name. Shawan, I'm Sandy, and this is Julie…..and….we seem to have lost our room keys."

"No problem ladies, I'll just issue two more. But if you find the others, would you return them?" answered Shawan, most obligingly.

"Sure," we replied in unison.

In our haste to get additional room keys, we had forgotten to transfer our clothes to the dryer. Back to the laundry room, out came the clothes from one washer, and promptly into another. Yes. We mistakenly put the clothes in a washer, inserted our money, and turned it on. Again. We were washing our clothes for the second time. Water flowed immediately, and we just looked at each other.

"WTF!" said Julie

"I can't believe we just did that. I mean both of us. Wouldn't you think one of us might have noticed that the machine had no heat settings?" I added.

"You know what? We're tired. Let's just go up to the room, and we'll come down later to dry them," said Julie.

We spent the next hour checking our social media. Yes. Email, Facebook, Instagram. Amazing that we still had the time and energy to hike, after keeping up with all of our following. I offered to go back to the laundry room, because it certainly didn't take two of us, and I didn't want my knee to get stiff. Plus, my hip hurt if I sat too long. Back I went, made the successful transfer, and knocked on our room door.

"Use your key, I'm in the bathroom," yelled Julie.

"Uh.....I don't seem to have it."

"Sandy, I saw you take them off the desk. I wondered why you needed both," said Julie.

"OK. This is getting weird. The keys aren't where I put them, and I don't remember taking them," I said, very puzzled.

Dementia? Really? Sudden onset?

"I guess I need to go back to the desk and get another set. Shawan is going to think we're senile," I said, figuring that since I lost this next set, I should be the one to get them.

"Hi Shawan. You're not going to believe this, but I've actually lost the fucking room keys again," I said, probably just a wee bit louder than was necessary with an inappropriate emphasis on my expletive.

Shawan was very gracious. But then, what could he really say. I was polite. It wasn't like I wanted to keep losing room keys. I promised to guard the next set with my life. So much for empty promises. Don't ask me to explain how it happened, but on the fourth visit to the desk, Shawan handed us five room keys. Yes. Julie went with me that last time. Miraculously, none of the five were lost by checkout time, and we managed to dry our clothes. I was thinking, get me back to the trail.

Julie spent a very long time studying the trail guide that evening and suggested we hike a section out of sequence, since I had my car. In other words, there was a very flat section around Boiling Springs where we could get on and off the trail after a day hike. All we would need to carry was our food and water. When we completed the section, which according to the guide was about seven miles, we would get off and hitchhike back to where we'd left my car. That way, she explained, it would give my knee and hip a lighter day, and we would still get some mileage. It sounded like an excellent idea to me, as I reapplied ice packs to both my knee and hip. Also, she suggested that we make a trip to Walmart before hitting the trail the next morning so she could pick up a few things.

The term AT hikers use for not carrying a full pack, is slack-packer. If you are one of the thru-hikers doing the entire trail in one block of time, this opportunity doesn't often present itself. It can, however, if you somehow manage to get access to transport-ation and lodging off the trail. For example, maybe you have some friends who are going to meet up with you. They would have a vehicle and a place to stay. You leave your gear with them, take enough food and water for the day, and you hike your section. They get you on and off the trail, you travel lightly, and get a bit of a reprieve. Because Lucy was with us, and we had no aversion to hitchhiking, or calling for a ride, we would slackpack the next day. Getting twenty-five pounds off my back sounded like an excellent plan to me.

Chapter 10: The Allenberry: Sunday, July 10

Every day that I check out the notes I took during my AT adventure, I am transported back there. It's summer again, and I'm on the trail. Some of the memories are just a little blurred, but for the most part, writing this is like hiking without the pack. What started out as somewhat of a chore, counting pages, setting arbitrary deadlines for myself in my recent world of retirement, has become that part of the day to which I most look forward. I would certainly rather write/type than iron. Or, bring in the wood, vacuum, dust, cook, or even sew. Writing this is my AT hike part of the day. I think that when I finish, I am going to need to hike another section. And maybe take better notes.

After breakfast and checkout, I sheepishly returned the five room keys to a puzzled desk clerk. Shawan was off duty. I explained the issue of repeated key loss, but she still gave me a pretty strange look. We found the local Walmart with no problem. I did not think I would be spending any of my allotted AT time in Walmart. It's not my favorite store. Can I just say, I really, really hate shopping there? But, we didn't have a lot of time, and it was the nearest place that would afford Julie all of the amenities she'd learned she had either forgotten to pack or didn't realize would be useful. For me, I must confess that I did make a couple of purchases. I bought a pair of flip flops to use as camp shoes because the thong thingy had popped out on one of mine. And I needed a better pillow than the one I'd brought. Screw the weight, how heavy can a pillow be? I could roll it up tightly to fit on the top of my pack.

Purchases made, we struck out for Boiling Springs and got lost. Several times. Pennsylvania is just not very generous with their signage. And we are not very adept at plugging in the GPS. We saw only one sign, and that was right before we entered the town. We did manage to find the Allenberry Resort Inn and Playhouse quickly, which was where we planned to stay that night. It would also be where we would leave Lucy parked. This place was amazing, with multiple well maintained buildings, manicured lawns, flowers, and the feel of luxury. Julie told me that they catered to hikers and had a special deal of forty dollars a night. I remember googling it. I actually called to check out the price because it just seemed too good to be true. They confirmed the forty dollars, and it made me suspect that they might have a barn or bunkhouse for the hikers with a communal shower.

Such was not the case, but neither did it appear especially welcoming to anyone. Actually, the place felt deserted. We drove around the grounds seeing very few parked cars. Initially, we saw no people. Parking, we walked up to check out a couple of the buildings, but they were locked. And clearly had not been used for their intended purpose in quite some time. One building looked like a huge banquet hall, all of the chairs were stacked, tables stood in rows with table cloths, but no dishes. Ditto for the building marked "Playhouse." There were still signs hanging outside advertising entertainers and plays, but none of these had recent dates.

"Jule, this is weird. It's like a ghost town. I can't imagine how we can stay here. I just talked to someone a couple of weeks ago, and she sounded like there would be no problem. What do you want to do?" I asked.

"I know what you mean. Let's see if we can find someone who works here. There's got to be somebody because there are some cars," answered Julie.

Getting back into Lucy, we drove around until we found a woman who appeared to be part of either the maintenance or housekeeping staff. Greeting her politely, we asked about hiker accommodations. She explained that the place had just been sold. She did mean *just*. Within the past few days it had changed hands, and the new management was in the process of making changes.

And, to our dismay, the new owner just left, which meant we would be unable to stay there for the night. The pleasant house-keeping lady told us she had to have permission to check in guests, even hikers. Maybe it was the look of disappointment accompan-ied by panic on our faces, but suddenly this woman seemed to have an epiphany.

"Ladies, if I can reach her by phone and she gives me per-mission, I could check you in. It would just be for one night, and I need cash," the woman explained.

"OMG! That would be so great if you could do that," Julie blurted out.

Those were my sentiments exactly. She just beat me to saying it aloud. It was like some sort of miracle happening to us. Here we go from finding this amazing place, to being told we can't stay, to actually having hope. The thing is, we needed to find a place to stay before we started hiking that day just in case we ran late. We didn't want to be out driving to the next town looking for a motel or a campground. The only other place in Boiling Springs was a bed and breakfast, and we didn't really want to do that if we could find something else. It would likely be pricey, and we really did have our sights set on forty dollars for tonight.

Our cleaning lady angel was able to reach the new owner, and she agreed to allow us to be checked in. We happily paid in cash which was fine with us. However, I did have a moment of panic where I thought I had been robbed because the cash I had remain-ing on me was not what I expected to find. After taking a deep breath, counting my money and doing a bit of mental math, which for me is a challenge because I am sort of math-impaired, was able to account for my cash-outflow. Bottom line, I had spent more than I planned on and brought less than I should have. I was able to pay my share of the upcoming night, so was OK.

You're probably wondering why I would panic at all, why I wouldn't just go to an ATM, which is what Julie had initially sug-gested. Well, that certainly sounds like a simple solution. That would of course, be assuming I actually had an ATM card, which I did not. I know. Pitiful. Hey, I only got a smartphone two weeks ago. The only reason I didn't get a flip phone was because our local Verizon store didn't have any. They told my husband and I they would have to special order them. Then the salesman started rolling out all of the discounts and making it seem like it really wouldn't cost any more, which of course, it did. In fact, turns out the monthly bill will be substantially larger. But the salesman was good at his profession, pointing out all the features of the new phone, assuring us of the simplicity in using it and how pleased we would be with this new modern miracle of communication and information resource.

I don't have to tell you that change is difficult. It's tough for anyone to make changes even when they are positive. It is especially difficult for my husband, particularly pertaining to electronics. John certainly does well when compared to his age-mates. The man is nearly eighty-two years old, looks sixty, and acts forty. Yes. He is very different from me. I am nearly sixty-two, look everyday of it plus a few more, and I'm not exactly sure what age I act like. Some days it's sixty, some days is sixteen. Sometimes, it depends upon how much wine I've drunk.

Regarding John and electronics, which include computers, ipads, radios, TVs, CD and DVD players, the heater in his truck, and flip phones as well as the new smartphone, there are ongoing issues. He manages these devices with what I would term as a minimum of competence. I do mean minimum. He gets by most days with some tech support generally from me, which in itself is a little scary. Although I am better with the devices that he is, that isn't especially noteworthy. So, I just knew that the new smartphone was going to present some challenges to me, and it was going to be nearly insurmountable for John. Texting for him would likely never, ever happen. In a convoluted manner of explanation, I think I have presented a pretty clear picture of why I didn't have an ATM card. John doesn't have one either. This could change.

We've got the phones, maybe we will step up and get the cards. I am optimistic. But for this AT trip I had only what was left of the one hundred dollars in cash I left home with and my credit card.

After handing over our forty dollars to the housekeeping lady, she showed us to our room. The building designated for hikers was definitely of *steerage caliber*. If you think of the Titanic and where the passengers with little money were crammed below deck, that gives subtle comparison to our room here at the Allenberry Resort. Our room was not of *resort caliber*. Actually, if we were migrant farm workers, we would likely be staying in a room like the one where we now found ourselves standing. I will concede that it was clean and did not smell of cigarette smoke. Probably the last time any sort of upgrade was made regarding paint, wallpaper, carpet, curtains, bedspreads, etc. was maybe 1970. But, as I mentioned, it was clean. The hot water faucet in the bathroom worked (we checked), and the toilet flushed. The big old TV with the fat back worked, and the place had cable. We were good. This would be fine. Well worth the forty dollars. Hey. We had just come off the trail. We were good here.

Once we settled in, we sorted through our gear, loading enough snacks, water, and a few miscellaneous items into our packs for the day hike we'd be taking. Our Walmart expedition and room securing mission took longer than expected, and it was now just about noon, lunch time. Can I just say, that never in my life have I tried to pack in extra calories to a meal. But here I was gobbing on butter and cream cheese to the bread for my tuna sandwich, wishing I had more of each and some mayo as well. It may sound gross, but it actually tasted really good. Hiking, even with a lightened pack, burns thousands of calories. This activity sure ain't for the weak, squeamish, and really skinny.

We had no problem finding the blaze marking the trail. It was almost across the road from the entrance to The Allenberry. We ran into the British couple, Slosh and Scavenger, who were headed there. We informed them of the precarious check-in situation, but they didn't seem particularly concerned. I suppose if we had come from across the Atlantic, secured visas, and hiked since April coming up from Georgia, we wouldn't give much thought to whether we could find the housekeeping lady to check in, either. Consulting our trail guide, we found a campsite catering to hikers in the area as well, so they would be OK if they were not able to secure a room.

I was really, really liking this section of the trail. The greatest appeal to me, my aching hip and sore knee, was the flat terrain. Not only was it flat, but it offered variety. Julie took a great picture of me, as I stopped to pet a horse while crossing a field. The horse was grazing and obviously used to hikers because he didn't even pick his head up while I stroked him. At least I think it was a him. I didn't examine the rear quarters. I like this picture of me for several reasons. I am a crazy animal lover, so of course any photo that shows me with a critter is a keeper. The pack on my back and hiking poles in my hands make me look like a hiker who knows what she is doing, even though she is relatively clueless. The fact that it is taken from a distance shows no trace of the wrinkly road map that has become my face. I look good in this photo taken from a respectable distance. I put it on Facebook right away. Maybe I will blow it up and frame it when I get home. Yeah! I liked it that much!

I sure enjoyed trekking across the pastures with the lightened load. The day was sunny and of course hot as hell, but I didn't mind it as much today. Julie said the same thing. This was her first time slackpacking, and after that first week she had spent on the trail with a pack so heavy she could hardly get it on her back, this was a definite reprieve.

"Jule, this is so cool! I love this part of the trail. I need to bring John down here. I think he'd like this."

"I know. Jamey said this was a really nice section," said Julie.

Perhaps I should have talked more about Jamey sooner, since he is the man who inspired Julie to hike. Although she has never met him in person, they communicate through social media. Jamey hiked thirteen hundred miles of the trail, but his adventure came to an abrupt end when he injured his knee and required surgery.

When Julie asked him what it had been like, forced to come off the trail before he could complete it, he told her: "It was like watching your child move out of the house for the first time. A moment of pride in what you had accomplished in raising your child mixed with the overwhelming desire for your child to never leave. That feeling never leaves you. The trail, like the thoughts of your children, never leaves you. The bond is so strong it sometimes makes it hard to breathe."

When Julie told me that, it gave me goosebumps. Having spent just a couple of days out on the trail was giving me a new perspective on life and the things our culture and society places value upon. I could actually almost understand his reaction to leaving the trail behind, not knowing if he would ever be able to return.

Jamey lives in our area and has been Julie's Wikipedia of hiking. He is her personal go-to-reference-manual, encouraging her all the way, making suggestions, and giving advice. She checks with him often when she has questions about the trail, which is several times a day, every day. I am too poorly informed about the trail to even know what questions to ask.

On an interesting sidebar, Jamey was actually an extra in one of the scenes from the movie, *A Walk In the Woods,* that featured Robert Redford and Nick Nolte. It's based on the book by Bill Bryson, which I did actually read even before Julie got the hiking idea. I loved the book and the movie. Although we are women and a bit older than the characters Nolte and Redford play, there is a hint of similarity. Julie did the research about preparing for this hike, talked to various hikers, and so had a fair idea of what she was getting herself into doing. On the other hand, although I am not an overweight recovering alcoholic who started the trip with an

overstuffed pack and lost a shoe, I am definitely more Stephen
Katz, the Nolte character. Julie is similar to Bill Bryson, played by
Robert Redford. Yeah. I didn't, nor do I presently, know much
about what I signed on to do. But here we are, trudging along,
enjoying the day, and having ourselves an adventure.

"Jule, do you think we'll have any trouble hitching a ride back
to The Allenberry?" I asked, as we crossed yet another field.

"Naw, Jamey says that people pick up hikers all the time. It's
pretty common to see them, especially near a town, when they
need to get off the trail and buy more supplies. Besides, we're
women. Should be no problem for us," she answered.

"Yeah, well this is maybe where my gray hair will help. See?
Not coloring can be good for something besides making you look
old, right?" I joked.

We hiked on, sweating, talking, laughing and stopping occasionally to rest, snack and drink water. I liked when the water
bottles were emptied because that made my pack lighter. We were
both looking forward to dinner since we were staying near town
and had the car, distance would not matter. It also meant we
wouldn't be eating a freeze dried meal. Nearing the end of our
seven mile section, we met up with a man and woman walking
with a yellow lab through a field.

"Ohhhh….a dog," I said, as we approached the couple.

Holding my hand out for the obviously friendly beast to smell,
I oogled and oggled at him. We stopped and chatted for a few
minutes, made introductions, and were soon engaged in a very
detail-sharing conversation with Dave and Janice.

"Have you guys ever seen the movie, *A Walk in the Woods*?
You know, the Robert Redford film that came out recently?" I
asked.

"Why yes, we really enjoyed it. Our daughter has done quite
a bit of hiking on the trail, and we take day hikes, so we're pretty
familiar with this section of it," replied Janice.

"Well, I'm the female version of the Katz character Nick

Nolte plays, minus the alcohol problem and packing too much gear. Julie is the hiker. She's spending the summer out here. I'm just joining her for about a week, but I'm more of a fish than a mountain goat. I swim a lot better than I hike," I explained.

"We're slackpacking for the day because Sandy fell yesterday and hurt her knee. We thought we'd try this flat section today. Actually, her car is at The Allenberry Resort, so we'll be hitch-hiking when we get to the highway. According to the trail guide, it's about two miles from here," explained Julie.

With a look of shock and horror etched into her face and genuine concern in her voice, Janice exclaimed, "Oh my, no one really hitchhikes around here. I don't think you'll be able to get a ride."

It was clear that she did not think hitchhiking was any kind of good idea. We persisted in our optimistic view of the ride pros-pect.

"Really, Janice is right. You won't be able to get a ride. People just don't do that around here. It's not that far out of our way, and we don't have any plans after our walk. We'll be glad to meet you at the road and drive you to town. Our daughter lives there. It's not a problem," said Dave, pretty forcefully

"Oh no," we both said nearly in unison.

"We can't ask you to do that. Really, I don't think we'll have a problem. I figure my gray hair will help. It's not like we look threatening," I said.

"Sandy's right. We'll be fine. But thanks so much for the offer," said Julie.

"Ladies, we don't mind. We're glad to help out. Please, it isn't a problem. Look, you're probably an hour from the road. Once you get there, just turn left and start walking. I'll be coming along in a black pickup. It has a back seat, so there's no problem fitting both of you in. It's only a couple of miles from there into town. We can show you where the restaurants are, too," said Dave.

Hmmm. Back seat in a pickup? Likely with seat belts? This was shaping up to be a vast improvement over our last ride. Plus, these folks presented as so very nice. And, normal. Why not? What's the worst that could happen? OK. So you are probably thinking serial-killer-rapists. But, seriously. How often does that really happen? And sometimes in life, as one grows old, old, and older, the ability to read people becomes a finely tuned skill. Like a human radar device. You can pick up the crazy vibes from the crazy people. Our ride back in Caledonia State Park with Larry and Bob had certainly turned out fine. Dave and Janice exuded with normal and kind. What the hell. This ride sounded good.

We looked at each other, looked at Janice and Dave, and agreed to accept their very, very generous offer. There we parted ways and headed for Route 11.

"Oh my God, Jule, can you believe this? What luck! They seem really pretty OK, don't you think?" I asked.

"Hell, yes. It's just another one of the cool things that's happened on this hike. I keep meeting the nicest people. And it was pretty obvious they were very concerned about our hitchhiking. I can't picture any of our girlfriends doing this, can you?" asked Julie.

"The hike or taking the ride from the black pickup?" I asked

"Either one!" answered Julie.

No. I could not picture it. In fact, I couldn't really picture any of the men I knew doing this. The hike or taking the ride from the black pickup truck. Well. There was one person. My husband. He would totally do this. And, take the ride. Actually, when he and I first started dating, there was this canoe camping trip we took, also in Pennsylvania. We put our rig into the waters of Pine Creek, also known as the Pennsylvania Grand Canyon, paddled all day and camped in the middle of the rattlesnake capital of the east.

No. I did not know about the rattlesnakes at the time. I didn't know about canoeing, either. Other than nearly capsizing in a set of rapids and being nearly eaten alive by killer black flies, our trip was generally uneventful. However, once we reached the place where we would be pulling the canoe out of the water the next afternoon, we were confronted with the task of returning to John's Chevy S-10 pickup truck, some twenty-five miles away. So. What to do? Hitchhike. We grabbed the paddles, stuck out our thumbs, and within no time, got ourselves a ride. No problem. It was fun. Really. It was empowering.

Before leaving for the hike, when we discussed our upcoming quest, the comments we got were primarily centered on the lack of bathing facilities. The folks we know, both friends and family, for the most part, don't like the idea of stinking. Right up there with the stink factor is having to carry what basically amounts to your bedroom and kitchen on your back. People do generally seem to like the idea of taking a walk in the woods, providing they have adequate protection from insects and can be assured that no snakes will be crossing their paths. Or bears, coyotes, skunks, raccoons, porcupines, field mice, stinging insects. You get the picture.

The people we hang with wade in the shallow end of the pool when it comes to high adventure. They are content to paddle around where they can still touch bottom. Us? Shit, no. We plop ourselves smack into the center of the deep end, come up for air, and just start swimming! Our take has always been that sometimes you just have to trust your gut, and "go with the gusto." We just hoped that the gusto didn't turn to shit.

I definitely stepped up my pace once I knew we were guaranteed a ride at the end of our hike this afternoon. I got this burst of energy. Knowing that a hot shower, wine, and meal that didn't come out of a vacuum-sealed bag awaited us spurred me forward.

"Holy shit, Sandy! I didn't know you could move this fast!"

"Yeah. It's like I got a second wind. And my knee doesn't hurt. I'm glad we didn't do hills today."

"Can you believe that Janice and Dave offering us a ride like this? They really seemed worried about us hitchhiking," said Julie.

"I know. I think we sort of peaked their interest. I mean,

we're not the typical hikers. I think when we mention having kids, being nurses, and just the fact that we're older makes people wonder why we're doing this."

Reaching the main road that Dave described, we saw a black truck. Yup. There he was, waiting for us. He explained that Janice had forgotten about things she needed to do at home, so she sent her regards. We loaded our packs and poles and climbed in the truck. It was clean and new, possessing the requisite number of seat belts. Quite a contrast from Ida's rig. Dave was very pleasant to talk with and pointed out various local points of interest as we drove toward our destination of Boiling Springs.

Reaching the town, he showed us where the good restaurants were. That didn't take long because Boiling Springs is a small town and there were only two. Boiling Springs Tavern and Aniles. He delivered us as promised to The Allenberry Resort and told us about the recent sale, and how sad it was that the facility was not utilized like it once was. He also gave us his card and told us to be sure and call in the morning if we needed anything, assuring us that he and Janice weren't busy and would be glad to pick us up again tomorrow after our hike. We thanked him, and said we'd be fine. My knee was feeling better, so we would get back on the trail with our full packs.

For dinner, we chose Anile's Ristorante and Pizzeria. No alcohol here, but then we had our own little stash. We could stop after dinner for some mixers and have our after dinner cocktails. There was a small grocery store where we could get some orange juice and ginger ale. Classy chicks, right?

Anile's was clean, relatively busy, and staffed with one, yes one, waitress. She was no spring chicken. She had to be our age or pretty close to it. She looked exhausted. So much so, that we actually offered to help her out. Like, we could pick up our own drinks and dinners and maybe even take a few orders. Neither of us had ever worked as waitresses, but how tough could it be? We were AT hiker girls!

Carla declined. I don't remember her actual name, but Carla fits. She did appreciate our offer, however. When she brought me the wrong dressing on my salad, I figured what the hell. I didn't have the heart to send her back to the kitchen for yet one more trip. I sucked it up. At this point I would probably have eaten a bowl of grass with some vinegar poured on. My appetite had returned. The food was really excellent here. In fact, I would drive out of my way to eat at this place. It was that good. Carla also told us that normally she did not work alone, so service was generally much faster.

It was such a beautiful night, and we were so very stuffed full of pasta, that we decided to take a walk around the small lake where the springs emptied in the center of the little town. There were lots of benches, and I took along the bread we hadn't eaten so I could feed the ducks. Stopping at the grocery store, I bought mixers for our vodka, and we toasted our very excellent several days on the trail, along with whatever else was awaiting us. We talked about all the events of the past couple of days, remarking about how very fortunate we both were to have this opportunity to start a new adventure in our seventh decade. And we laughed out loud when we discussed the reactions most of our friends would be having if they had to dig a hole in the woods to poop.

"It's like we're trekking through nature's great big kitty litter box," I said to Julie.

Boiling Springs is a quaint and beautiful town located several miles southwest of Carlisle. There is a seven acre body of water in the middle called Children's Lake. It was there that we sat, sipping our after dinner drinks, and I fed the ducks, geese, and whatever other critter came within distance of my tosses. The lake was formed by partially damning the brook that is fed by some thirty natural springs. As in many small towns, there is a great deal of history contained for those interested enough to inquire.

Boiling Springs is famous not only for its unique system of wells, but also because of the iron works that developed there and dates back to pre-revolutionary times. These springs are not actually boiling in any place, unlike other areas with hot springs in the US. They just appear to be bubbling as the water is pushed to the surface. Actually, the water temperature is relatively constant throughout the year at 52 degrees F. If we had more time, we might have done a little more poking around, but we would be getting back on the trail in the morning, so that venture would have to wait for another day, another time.

Returning to our very dated room in the *steerage section* at The Allenberry, we turned on the TV for background noise, got into our pajamas and focused our attention on catching up with our social media postings. I think we were the only guests there, which certainly made for a quiet evening. Although it would have been nice to chat with a few fellow hikers regarding the most recent happenings on the trail, we were totally fine with the privacy and comfort of modern amenities.

Chapter 11: Trail Angels: Monday, July 11

As we were packing up to leave in the morning, Julie's phone rang. It was Dave and Janice, and they were offering to pick us up at the end of our hike and inviting us to stay at their cabin near Pine Grove Furnace tonight. We looked at each other, shrugged, and agreed to accept their hospitality. This would allow us yet another day of slackpacking which certainly wouldn't hurt my still very tender knee any. We made our plan to drive back to the Pine Grove Furnace General Store where I had cleaned up after my splat. There, we would leave Lucy, hike nine miles to Hunters Run Road, which was Route 34, and meet Dave and Janice at the store/deli. They would drive us back to Lucy, and we would follow them to their cabin, which they told us was very close to the General Store.

Well, this could be an interesting night. But, if we read this couple correctly, and I think that we did, we would have a very enjoyable evening of conversation. We were both taking a chance. They certainly didn't know exactly what we held in store for them, either, and they were really taking more of a gamble, because they were inviting us into their home. Think about what could happen. They could be religious fanatics who felt it was their mission to save us. Or, they could be raging alcoholics who would be in drunken stupors before the evening was over. They could be kinky, weird people. And from their vantage point, we could be those same things. We were all taking a chance on first impressions and gut feelings.

The nine miles of trail we hiked was relatively uneventful. We sweated, snacked, drank copious amounts of water, and devoted a considerable amount of our conversation to anticipating what Dave and Janice would be like as we got to know them more. We also discussed what we might expect from their cabin's accommodations. Reaching Route 34, Julie called and told them where we were. Shortly, Dave and Janice arrived, and once again, we piled in the backseat of the black pickup truck equipped with seat belts.

"Say, are there any restaurants near your cabin? We would be glad to treat you," I offered.

"Oh, you don't need to do that. We planned to have you ladies eat with us. We had company over the weekend, and it's leftovers, so if you don't mind that, we can eat out on our back patio," replied Janice.

Wow! This was amazing. Not only were they transporting us, they were going to house and feed us. This was not anything we were expecting.

"Are you sure? We don't want to inconvenience you. We'd be happy to treat you to dinner," Julie said.

"It's no problem. We have lots of food. And there really aren't any good places to eat that are close by. We would need to go back into town. It's too nice a night for that. We think you'll enjoy the cabin. We really love spending time there."

We gave up any more pretense of arguing and decided we would just climb on this roller coaster and see where it let us off. Just as Dave and Janice had offered, they drove us back to Lucy, parked at The General Store. As I recall, Julie rode with Dave, and Janice with me, so there was no chance of getting lost. We wound around a few back roads and about ten minutes later, we were pulling up to this beautiful, original with the white chinking, immaculately kept, log cabin. All we could both do was gape with our mouths open. What amazingly kind people! What a break for us! What an opportunity to restore some faith in humanity.

"Wow! This place is great! My husband would love it! He has always wanted to build and live in a log cabin…...I mean we love our house and all, but this is just so cool!" I said, unabashedly excited.

Although Julie already lives in a pretty amazing log cabin

herself, she, too, was impressed with the chinking, the character, the rustic setting, and the hospitality of our hosts. They gave us the tour and then ushered us out to the back patio, where Dave was already making preparations for grilling. Homemade wine was poured, snacks were set out, we plopped ourselves down and took a few deep breaths, and once again thanked them for their generosity.

It was easy conversation. They told us about their children and grandchildren, the area, their interests. We did the same. We laughed, we drank, we ate. And then the subject of the main dinner course came up.

"I hope you like chicken," said Janice, as she handed the plate of raw foul to Dave.

"Oh, I love chicken but Sandy might have a little problem," said Julie with a big twist of sarcasm.

"You aren't allergic, are you? I can always fix you something else," Janice said, worriedly.

"Oh, she's not allergic. She doesn't eat meat. I love meat. In fact, I hunt and even gut my own deer. Sandy tries to put a curse on me every year," laughed Julie.

"Well, actually, I try not to eat meat. I mean I try not to eat land creatures. I eat fish. But on this trip, I haven't exactly been pure. I told Julie I'd suck it up and eat chicken. It's just too hard to get enough calories, and the freeze dried stuff is mostly meat based. It's no problem. I can eat some chicken."

Now, egged on by Julie, Dave started talking about all sorts of meat dishes. And announced that he would be frying up bacon for breakfast. I announced I would be passing on the bacon, as I expounded on the wonders of pigs, their intelligence, and how I so wanted one for a pet. Our leisurely picnic dinner on Dave and Janice's patio lasted until dark. At that point we took the conversation on into the very cozy living room, and if we didn't need to get an early start in the morning, likely would have talked on until the early morning hours.

On just a little sidebar, a suggestion for hiking preparation that I forgot to mention in the beginning is to be sure your toenails are adequately trimmed. They should be cut as short as is comfortably and safely possible. Why do I know this? Because I had over-looked this small task, and mine were now protruding way past the ends of my cute little bony toes and ramming painfully into the ends of my hiking shoes. This was especially noticeable on the downhill treks. And I really looked forward to going downhill, because it was just so very much easier. But, now it was painful. Shit. Pain on the way up the hill from lugging the pack, pain on the way down from cramming my toenails into what felt like the concrete abutment of my shoe. I really did need to remedy this situation, and cutting them here, in a civilized indoor setting with adequate lighting provided by electricity would be way easier than out on the trail.

No. Julie does not know I got out my clippers, put on my reading glasses, spread several paper towels, and gave myself a mini-pedicure. She was seemingly occupied with catching up her Facebook followers on our progress. If she did know, there was no comment, and she pretended she didn't. I know if she was hacking away at her toenails, I would pretend not to notice. I would just leave the room. Ewwww. Gross. I know. Like peeing and poo-ing in the woods. Carrying your own little shovel, wrapped of course in some plastic, so as not to touch anything.

Come to think of it, I don't believe I have mentioned the part about poo burial yet. This is important information. Really. Think of it. We all pee, we all poo. There are no bathrooms on the trail, save for the outhouses near some of the shelters. So. What to do when one feels nature's call between shelters? It would get disgusting pretty quickly if folks just stepped off the trail and let things plop. Flies would gather, and on hot days the stench could be pretty overwhelming because there are a lot of hikers out here. Records at Harpers Ferry in December of 2015 showed that 1385 northbound hikers passed through that year. These stats don't include the section hikers, like me, who are only out for a short period of time. All of those people make for a whole lot of poo. Prevention of stink and flies and the just plain disgusting thought of stepping in another person's poo requires hikers to bury their stuff. Burying requires digging, which means a small shovel is needed. Yes. Hikers carry poo shovels. Me? Well, I have mentioned my concern with extra, unnecessary weight, and so I did not obey that unwritten rule. I'm not totally disgusting, however. I followed the burial ritual. I just used a stick. The stick worked fine. I dug the hole, I did my thing. I covered up. Personal grooming which had included showers, was complete. We spread our sleeping bags on top of the beds so that Janice wouldn't have to change the sheets, although she assured us it was no problem, and settled in for the night.

Chapter 12: Unsuccessful Hitchhikers: Tuesday, July 12

We woke up to the sound of voices and the smell of bacon frying. Although, as I mentioned, I could never eat the little pig, I have to admit that I don't mind the smell of bacon. I would like to say I am appalled and grossed out, but sadly, I am not. It smelled really good. Not good enough, however, to get me to eat any.

We found Janice in the kitchen, where the coffee was brewing, and a bowl of pancake batter sat on the counter. She was adding blueberries, and Dave was manning the grill on the patio, tending to the bacon.

"Good morning, ladies. Did you sleep OK? What time would you like to be on the road? Or, should I say trail," asked Dave.

"Wow! You didn't have to go to all of this trouble for breakfast," said Julie.

They had even started a campfire. Who eats breakfast on the patio with a campfire? It's something you might read about and want to do, but just never quite get around to doing it. Plus, actually having a patio, grill, and fire pit are all helpful. Suddenly, I came up with a way of paying back Dave and Janice for their very generous hosting of us. I had several slates in my car, all wrapped up nicely, with nature scenes sketched in black ink. Dale, a very arty friend of mine was always looking at venues to sell his work. John and I bought one of a beautiful butterfly, and I'd taken several others with me to try and sell over the summer. There was one especially nice drawing of a moose. Hmmm. A moose would just fit the décor of this cabin perfectly. I'll buy it and leave it as a thank-you. Actually, no. I won't just leave it. I'll get it out of the car and give it to them.

I thought Janice was going to cry. They both absolutely loved the moose and hung him next to their front door. I couldn't think of a better place for Mr. Moose, and Julie agreed. This gesture lessened the guilt we were beginning to feel for all of the services this very nice couple had been providing for us.

Because Lucy was with us and Dave and Janice were still up for being a transport service, Julie and I were afforded yet one more day of slackpacking. We came up with a plan whereby we would leave my car with Janice. Dave would drive us back to where he picked us up on Route 34, and we would hike the eleven miles on into Boiling Springs. Janice would leave Lucy at her daughter's house, and she gave us directions of where to find it. Boiling Springs was such a small little town, she assured us we would have no problem finding the house, since it was very near Caffe 101, where we had eaten breakfast several days ago.

I was beginning to wonder how it would be when I once again had to wear the full backpack, but for now, decided to just enjoy yet one more day of reprieve. I carried the thing before, I would carry her again. Although I have not yet named my backpack, I do think of her as female. Why, I'm not sure. I have a history of naming inanimate possessions, and it doesn't appear that I have established any rationale for why I assign the names I do. My mountain bike was called Mr. Ed. I've named my Subaru Forester, Lucy. I also named my kayak, Lucy. My other cars have been nameless, as have my other bikes. I'm not sure what gear kicked in that has me naming things. Perhaps it's age. Or, maybe my daughter has influenced me. She has been naming vehicles since high school.

Shortly into this hiking gig, I began studying the trail guide very closely. I wanted to know where the hills were going to be, how long between streams, and what I could expect of the terrain. I am one who likes to know what to expect. Yes. One could say that I have *control issues*. I want to prepare myself. I am organized, pragmatic, and always thinking of a plan B for any situation. Given that I tend to have a bit of a problem with anxiety, I'm not sure if this is especially helpful, but I tell myself that it's better to know what's coming. I would look at where we hiked, assess how difficult the terrain was for me, and look ahead so that I could be prepared for the next hill. In my world they were mountains, but when I looked at the actual elevation, I had to admit they were not. After this trip was over, I would be telling people they were mountains. Why not? What did they know?

The section of today's hike that had my attention and was causing me concern and anxiety was called Rock Maze, and there were two of them, side by side. The trail winding through Pennsylvania is notorious for rocks, and we already discovered this was something to be considered. The rocks made walking very precarious so it was constant vigilance watching where to plant your feet. If we got any rain, that would make these nuggets of peril slippery, and navigating them was tough enough when they were dry.

Now, when I say rocks, I refer to boulders as well. And, I do mean very big, huge boulders. Climbing between and over them requires concentration because one slip can result in a serious injury. And if not serious, one that at least knocks you off the trail, like spraining or breaking an ankle, an arm, cracking your skull. You get the picture. Caution is important. The rock maze totally had my attention. But, fortunately, it was toward the beginning of our hike, about four miles in. That was good because we wouldn't be tired yet.

This was another hot, sticky day. About two miles into the hike, we came upon Footbridge Stream. This was one of the largest streams we'd come across and as had become my habit, I took off my shirt, dipped it in the water, wrung it out, and put it back on. Next, I splashed water on my head and face, soaking my hair. I also soaked my green bandanna and wrapped it back in place around my head. I looked better with the headband thing than my safari hat. I was taking Julie's word for that fashion assessment. We rested for a few minutes, because according to the trail guide the rock mazes were coming up soon.

I have never, ever seen such huge boulders. At least the trail was well marked, or so we thought, through this treacherous section. Up, up, up we climbed. We remarked about how glad we were to not have full packs. Up, up, up some more, and then, finally, the trail wound back down. Knowing there was another maze, we moved slowly. Soon, we found ourselves at yet another rather large stream, with a footbridge. Amazing. Two of these within about a mile of each other.

"Jule, what are you doing with the compass?"

"I think we just made a big circle. Doesn't this look familiar?" she answered.

What did I know. It all looked pretty much the same to me. Rocks, trees, streams, if the trail wasn't marked with the white blazes, I would have no idea where to go. And I have to confess, that in all of my sixty-one years, I have never read a compass. Call me direction retarded, impaired, challenged, whatever the current politically correct terminology. That is what I am. I pay attention if my situation really requires it, otherwise, I am pretty oblivious.

Somehow, somewhere, we missed a blaze on the trail. So far they had been clear and easy to spot. We never found ourselves at a loss for determining where the path was going. We didn't have to concentrate on locating the blazes. Nothing had been different today. It was no hotter, no less sunny, we were rested, hydrated, and fed. Except that somehow, somewhere in that first rock maze, we got turned around. We apparently descended when we should have gone left or right.

"Shit," said Julie.

"Fuck," I followed with.

"I don't know where we went wrong," said Julie.

"Those rocks were a bitch to climb. What if we end up right back here again?" I asked.

"I know. I'm not sure what we should do."

I knew that I did not want to climb that mini Mt. Everest again. I suggested backtracking and getting on the first main road, where we could hitch a ride back to our car in Boiling Springs.

Julie dug the trail guide out of her pack, and we both studied it, deciding that my backtracking idea was the most sensible thing to do. It looked like the main road was about three miles from the footbridge stream where we were now standing, or in my case, sitting. I had removed my shoes and socks and was soaking my feet in the icy cold water. Considering we already completed a loop with the first rock maze, it appeared we had hiked about four miles already.

It was hot, hot, hot and humid, not the kind of day where a hiker would want to climb up a steep maze of rocks any more times than necessary. Looking at the guide, we found that the closest town was Mount Holly Springs, which was on Route 94. Good. There would be a decent amount of traffic since the town was so close. We should have no problem hitchhiking back to Lucy in Boiling Springs. Who wouldn't take pity on two mature women with backpacks and hiking poles? My white/gray hair stood out like a beacon of need. Clearly, we were not threatening. Pathetic, maybe. Threatening, no. We would have ourselves a ride in no time.

Trudging back along the trail we had just traveled, we kept trying to figure out where it was that we screwed up. The only thing we came up with was the trail at the top of the first rock maze. Looking back, there must have been a blaze we missed. Maybe we were distracted by talking. Whatever the reason, we had screwed up. At this point it didn't matter. We made a wrong turn, hiked in a big circle, were hot, sweaty, and discouraged. My time on the trail was nearing the finish line and making wrong turns would not help me build my resume of trail miles.

Seeing the highway in the distance caused us to quicken our pace. Hey, we would be back to Lucy in no time and driving back out to the Allenberry Resort, where we would spend the night. We would have a bed, shower and another restaurant meal. What wasn't to like? This was all good. I think this was the hottest day yet, although I've said this every day of the hike. Maybe each day added a couple of degrees. Whatever the present temperature, which was well into the nineties, and extremely humid, we were cooking. Walking along the road with the sun beating down on the concrete, just added a couple more degrees. Nice. Just what was needed. My back was getting achy from the unforgiving surface. Dirt trails are much kinder. Yeah, the rocks were tough, but there was enough soft earth in between to offset that.

"Wait a minute. If we're going to be out in the sun, I need to put on more sunscreen. I have serious damage control to do here. And I better lose the headband and put my hat back on."

I dug out my tube of Badger #30 SPF sunscreen and applied it liberally to my face and forearms. I didn't bother to rub it in very well, because I was sweating so much, I figured I'd lose some of the protection. So, yes, my face was coated with thick, white, pasty zinc oxide. It looked like a baby's butt with deep creases.

Two years ago I stopped using the mainstream sunblocks because of all the chemicals they contained. Not only do I read food labels, I pretty much read all product labels that contain substances going in or on me. I found some very disconcerting information about oxybenzene and retinyl palmitate. Using products like these where the protection is absorbed into the skin can actually be harmful. The safer options are those containing the zinc oxide, which forms a barrier from the sun rays. Also, wearing loose clothing that covers exposed skin and a wide brimmed hat is recommended.

Let me just say, that when out hiking in ninety plus degree temperatures, covering up is not something that is appealing. I tried that the first day and nearly passed out from heat stroke. Covering up did not do it for me. So, being the ingredient elf that I am, my only reasonable option if I am not going to rub the chemicals into my skin, is to wear the pasty stuff. It isn't attractive, but at this point in my life, I have derailed from the fashion train and nixed the foundation makeup. I can't afford the quantities I would need to buy.

Once I was adequately covered, at least to my standards, we stuck out our thumbs. We were confident. We were upbeat. We were ready to put this mistake behind us. The ride would be happening anytime. We were ready to climb into some kind soul's vehicle. The traffic was nearly constant, and we were standing in a place where we were visible from a long distance away. There would be plenty of time to pull over safely. Except that this ride thing was not happening.

I was glad to not be carrying a full pack because as I mentioned, standing or walking on the concrete was much harder than hiking in the woods. I started to obsess about a lower back blowout, which has been my big fear throughout this hike. We decided that maybe our location could be a factor, so we set off, walking up the road, putting our thumbs out as we moved along. However, it really was not my thumb I wanted to extend. It was my middle finger. I did recognize that probably that wouldn't be the best way to secure a ride. Who wants to pick up someone who's telling them to fuck off? No one with whom you would likely want to climb into a car or truck.

After walking a distance of what seemed like ten miles, but was actually closer to one, we were beginning to understand why Janice and Dave reacted as they had when we told them about our plans to hitchhike. It was becoming painfully obvious that this activity was not popular here. We were getting very discouraged, but we plodded along. Finally, a small, rusty pickup truck slowed down and pulled up next to us. The young contractor-type guy very politely offered us a ride. Except that his truck was a two-seater. And, a small one at that. Cramming both of us into the passenger side didn't seem to be the best idea. Oh, how I longed for the days of my youth, when there was no problem with loading a group of people into the back of a pickup. It was like riding in a convertible. But, like my youth, and my creamy skin, those days are history. Right now, it seemed like ancient history.

"Jule, I don't think we should get in. It's illegal to ride like this in New York; I'd hate to cause this guy to get a ticket."

Looking longingly at the truck and pausing for just a moment, I just know she was thinking that maybe we could split up, and she could take this ride, since I was being so picky.

"Hey, thanks so much, but we don't want to be the reason you get a ticket. We shouldn't have a problem with someone else stopping. We really appreciate it, but we better not," I said.

"Uh, no problem," contractor-guy said.

The fact that he didn't argue told me two things. One, he wasn't some crazy kind of sex pervert murderer. Two, he was relieved we didn't take him up on his offer. He tried to do a good deed by offering, and we let him off the hook by refusing. I guess we both sort of won. Meanwhile, the ride scene was not looking good. Not even a little bit good. No one was even slowing down. I doubt anyone was looking at us. Though we weren't carrying full packs, they were heavy enough. This was not the type of day any sane person would choose to be walking along the shoulder of a state road for pleasure. If this scenario were to continue, we would be walking all the way to Boiling Springs. This was not what our plan for the day included. This was a good deal further than our bodies were wanting to walk, especially on the concrete.

So, we trudged along, sweating, grumbling about not getting picked up and very likely we stunk. I am not sure exactly what prompted her, but at some point, Julie seemed to feel the need to place some blame on me for the situation we were currently in. Like I wanted to be out here in rural Pennsylvania with my thumb stuck out under the blazing sun, getting even more damage to my lizard skinned face.

"You know, maybe if you didn't have that Freddy Krueger shit all over you face, we might have a chance. You're scaring people. You're even scaring me and I know you."

Oh my. That was direct. Without a mirror, there wasn't much I could say in my defense. Maybe she was right. Perhaps I had overdone the sunblock application thing just a little. All I could think to do was ask her just how wrinkly she expected me to get. But, I didn't. We generally get along so well. There was no point in having a major meltdown over Badger #30 SPF here on Pa Route 94.

"Is it that bad?"

"Yes! Didn't you ever see those Freddy Krueger horror movies? How much of that shit do you need? Can't you just pull down your hat brim?"

I guess she had a point. What would I do if I saw two women walking along the side of the road with their thumbs stuck out and one of them wearing what appeared to be a white mask? I might think they were trying to disguise themselves. Maybe they were criminals. At the very least, I'd likely think there was some sort of mental illness involved. I might be concerned about the white shit getting on my car upholstery, too.

"Well, maybe I could rub it in some more, so you can't see it. I guess I might have overreacted to the sun just a little. Wait up here while I get some off."

I rubbed, and rubbed, and rubbed, wiping the excess on my pants. She was right. There really was a lot of white goop on my face. I also had to admit, it felt better, too. It was like I'd splatted on half a dozen layers of foundation-pancake-makeup.

"That's way better. At least I can look at you now. Sandy, the scary cream is way, way worse than any of your wrinkles. They aren't that bad. You can't even see them until you get really close."

"Are you sure? I wish I'd listened to my mother. She told me and told me how bad the sun was for my skin. She gave me articles, she showed me pictures, and I just ignored her. I wanted the tan, you know? I mean, I'm eastern European. I am one of those people who freckle and glow after I burn and peel. You know, I have more wrinkles than my mom. And more gray hair. She's ninety-two. I'm screwed. Good thing I still look OK from a distance."

Julie laughed out loud at that one. I guess that meant we were OK. I was doing my part. I made myself presentable. Maybe now a ride would soon be awaiting us. We decided to continue walking up over a hill that had a sharp curve in it, figuring there was no way anyone would be able to pull over there, even if they wanted to give us a ride. We spotted a woman working in her garden across the road and ventured over to ask for directions to Mount Holly Springs. We were also thinking that just possibly, she might offer us a ride. She gave us directions. She did not offer a ride. And we didn't mention that we were actually hitchhiking.

We walked on. We kept our thumbs out and our spirits up. Well, they were sort of elevated. The farther we walked, the more we grumbled, but we weren't totally losing hope for finding a ride. After what seemed like an abbreviated eternity, we reached Mt. Holly Springs, a cute little town. What we really wanted to do was stop for a cold beer and just check into a motel, hope for a hot tub and call it a day. But, because as I previously mentioned, my time on the trail was running out and I would be returning to the chaos of everyday life soon enough, we started looking earnestly for the prospect of a ride. Our pride was gone, as was our hygiene, though we didn't seem to stink very much; at least I couldn't smell Julie. We do tend to have a great deal of tolerance for our own foul odor. Still, although we were gritty and very sweaty, the odor wasn't there. Yet.

That point would be significant when it came to securing a ride. No one wants to put a stinking person in their vehicle, even if it already stinks. I guess there is something about introducing new foulness to the upholstery of your car. At any rate, we were starting to feel a little desperate, because time was passing, and Boiling Springs was several hours away by foot on the highway.

"Jule, I think we should just ask someone for a ride. What can they say? No? WTF! We'll just ask someone else."

"Yeah, that sounds good to me."

"We need to look for someone with a decent car, somebody

who looks pretty squared away. We don't want a creepy pervert. And we want a car with seat belts. No rusty pickup with a gun rack," I specified.

"I have a gun rack," stated Julie.

"I know. But you're a girl. And your truck isn't rusty. Well, your car, I mean. You really have a rack in that new car of yours?" I asked, genuinely curious.

"Well, no, it isn't in my car. I just have a gun rack."

"It's not a problem when people have them in their house. Shit. I have a gun rack. At least I did. I gave it to Jamie when my dad died. My shotgun's standing in a cemetery vase in my living room, and my BB gun's in my sewing closet. I don't worry about the guns people have in their houses. I just worry when they hang them in their trucks. Or cars. That creeps me out."

"I didn't know you had a gun," said Julie.

"Yeah. Remember those times we shot skeets at the local rod and gun clubs? And I even hit a couple of them?"

"It's skeet. No s on it. Oh yeah. I do remember. I thought that was your father's gun."

"It was. He gave it to me."

"How come he didn't give it to your brother?"

"I dunno. Gary got all the other guns. Did you know my dad used to take them apart and refinish them? It was a hobby for awhile. He'd look for different types of old guns. Like from other countries. Kinda cool, don't you think? He never shot any of them. Never had any ammunition."

"Oh. No, I never knew that about your dad. I knew he made the wood things, like the crates and that Christmas stable you gave me."

"Yeah, he sure did like to work with wood. He always got a kick out of the stuff you made with your scroll saw."

Julie actually had her own shop. A *she shed* before its time. She made decorative things like dogs, cats, and apples, painted them, put hooks on the back, and hung them up. For several years, she gave them out as presents, and I still have the mama and baby pig hanging in my kitchen. In fact, as I remember, after my dad saw her stuff, he got a scroll saw and started turning out the craft projects. He'd saw and sand; my mom would paint. They gave a lot of little wooden critters out as gifts, and I still have some of them hanging or standing in my house. My dad worked in a corner of our basement and would have loved a shop of his own like Julie had.

I remember him often remarking, "That Julie's got her own shop; don't see many women with their own shop." Yeah. He was envious.

"Hey, check out the guy getting out of his car. The one with the white hair. He looks pretty safe. His car's clean. Looks pretty new. Maybe he'd like to help out a couple of stranded women," I said, hopefully.

"You ask," said Julie.

She knows I am so not short on nerve. I will talk with anyone. Granted, I'm not the interviewer my husband is, but I do alright. We walked over to him and caught up just before he crossed the street.

"Excuse me sir, we're trying to get to Boiling Springs. We got turned around on the trail today, and we need to get back to our car," I said.

And then Julie blurted out, "Is hitchhiking even legal here?"

Now, all dignity lost, I whined, "No one will pick us up."

We both sounded like we were near tears. We weren't, but this man didn't know that. He got a little flustered, but answered us politely.

"No, not so far as I know. Course, we don't see many hitchhikers around here."

"Boy, that's for sure. How do people get back and forth on the trail?" I asked.

"I don't know about that," answered the man, who now seemed to be in a hurry.

Likely he was in a hurry to get away from us. I think we were scaring him. It wasn't my face anymore, either, because I had taken Julie's suggestion and wiped the sunscreen off.

"Do you know where we could get a ride to Boiling Springs? We'll pay," I said.

The scared man looked at his watch. "Look, I'm going to get a haircut here," he said, pointing to the barber shop directly across from where we were standing. "If you don't mind waiting, I'll run you over after that. And I don't need any money. This will be my good deed for the day."

"Great," we said, actually in unison. We were so so very relieved.

"Where should we meet you? Just back here by your car?" I asked.

"Sure. I should be back in about half an hour."

"Jule, we got ourselves a ride! In a nice car! Can you believe it?"

Less than five minutes passed, and the scared man walked toward us, with keys in hand.

"It's crowded in there. Tell you what. I'll just run you gals over to Boiling Springs, then I'll come back here and get my haircut. Place should be thinned out by then."

We made general small talk as we drove. He seemed to be a nice enough man, and we were certainly grateful that he decided to make us the target of his good deed for the day. I can't recall specific details about our driver other than the fact that his car was very clean. Turns out it was about six miles to town, which was less than we calculated, but more than we wanted to walk on pavement at that point. He dropped us off right at our car, which had been parked by Janice, as promised, in front of her daughter's house. It was just so nice to see Lucy again! Loading our packs and poles into the back, we plopped our tired asses in and wound our way up to The Allenberry Resort. It would be so nice to check back into that dated room, with the clean bathrooms and comfy mattresses.

Except this did not seem to be happening for us. Driving around the grounds as we had done before, produced not a single person in view. It was like a ghost town. Or maybe The Twilight Zone. I mean, there was nothing. No cars. No activity. Nothing. Beautifully maintained grounds and buildings with absolutely no live humans around. Anywhere. Getting out of the car, we walked around, looked in a few windows, and knocked on a few doors. Still, nothing and no one.

"Shit, Jule. What's going on?"

"I don't know. This is weird. It doesn't look like there are even maintenance people around. Somebody has to keep this place up. There has to be people here somewhere," said Julie.

We got back in Lucy, made another loop around and then saw a couple of cars with people standing next to them, talking. Maybe they were looking for a room, too, and would know who to ask. We pulled up next to them, got out of Lucy and inquired about lodging. They looked very annoyed. At us.

"Sorry, we're closed to lodging right now. The property just sold yesterday, and we're transitioning to new ownership," a guy standing next to his very nice, shiny, new pickup truck with no gun rack told us.

"But we just stayed here two nights ago. Down in that building," I said, pointing.

"We're Appalachian Trail hikers and were told that there was lodging here. It even says so in the trail guide," I continued, probably sounding as desperate as I was feeling.

"I told you, we're closed. Sorry. You need to find other lodging for the night," the guy said with an emphatic rudeness.

"Fuck you," I thought. "I won't stay here even if you re-open for guests. You're an asshole and you could have given us a room for tonight."

"Is there any other place in town?" asked Julie.

"Yeah, there's a Bed and Breakfast. That's the only place here unless you want to drive out toward Carlisle."

We climbed back into Lucy. Hot, tired, discouraged and getting hungry.

"Well, let's go to town. I think I remember seeing a sign for a B & B. Remember where we had that good breakfast the other morning? I think it's near there."

"Yeah, I remember seeing it. Looks like the house from The Addams Family. Or Munsters."

"That's it," I said.

So, we drove back to town and pulled up next to Gelinas Manor. It was a trip back into time. Clearly, in its day, it had been a magnificent show place. It's just that the time had passed. The time had passed long, long ago. Granted it wasn't that the vines and plants completely overran the outside, but it was sorely in need of a landscaping face lift. And the iron gate was ominous. This was not feeling like a cozy place. However, as that rude man had told us, this was it. Neither Julie nor I felt like driving back toward Carlisle at this point. Nor did we feel like tenting in the backpacker's campground.

Tomorrow would be our last full day on the trail, and the section we needed to complete was about eleven miles. We would need to get an early start and a decent night's sleep. The manor it would be for tonight, providing there was a room available. Upon looking up and down the streets on both sides of the corner where this albatross sat and seeing no other cars parked, we were reasonably sure there would be a room available.

We knocked on the door. We waited. Finally, a very, very elderly lady answered.

"Hi, we're wondering if you have a room available for the night. We were going to stay at The Allenberry, but were told they aren't taking guests right now. Something about it being sold," I said.

Silence. Staring. The staring was coming from the manor keeper. I'm guessing it was Gelina. She not only stared, but there was some hostile glaring going on as well. Really? All we wanted was a room. Did we look that bad? Had we started to stink?

"One room?" asked glaring lady

"Uh, yes, just one room. We're hiking on the AT," I said, as if the fact that we were unkempt and toting backpacks didn't already state the obvious.

"You need to leave your packs outside. You can't bring them in. Not at any point. My cheapest room is ninety-nine dollars with a shared bathroom. You'll share the bathroom with me, so I expect you to be respectful. Breakfast is promptly served at 8:30, and I don't serve after that. You need to lock the door if you leave. How will you be paying?"

Well, well, well. Aren't we just the welcoming inn-keeper? Maybe driving to Carlisle wasn't such a bad idea. But, we didn't consider it. Looking at each other, we agreed to stay right here. Fuck the attitude and rules. We would answer with politeness. After all, she was older. Who knew just how old? Or, how well? We would take the high road, which always seems to be more challenging. But, we were tough. We were AT hiker girls.

Chapter 13: The Bed and Breakfast: Still July 12

This was the second last night of my adventure. Day after tomorrow, I would be returning to the hectic confusion of what life in the twenty-first century of rural Western New York State has become. Tonight would be sort of a prelude back to that because we were off the trail. We were in town.

Our innkeeper was warming up to us just a little more. I think the fact that we didn't stink or at least stunk at a tolerable level helped us. Plus, we mentioned a few tidbits about who we were: nurse, counselor, retired, married (we omitted Julie's impending divorce), mothers. The summation of which is that we really were very respectable women out for some adventure, looking to do something challenging before we were too feeble, tired, old, or dead. She remained a little wary and never did tell us to call her by her first name upon introductions. Hence, I shall refer to her as Sophia.

I was impressed that she was able to split the fee and charge each of our credit cards individually. Not many people in their eighties are especially literate when it comes to computers and the programs that might be used. My own husband generally manages if there is some tech support through me, kids, or grandkids. He is sort of OK until there is a problem. Like, if the internet goes down or he accidentally changes the font size. I wondered who provided tech support for Sophia. I noticed a lot of family photos hanging on the walls, so clearly there were some children involved.

Sitting in her office while the credit card transaction was being completed, we made some small talk. She told us that her son helped her out and wanted her to sell the business. However, even though her husband had been dead for some time, she just wasn't ready.

"What would I do? I'm not ready to leave my home. And, I

like having guests, as long as there aren't very many. Anymore, the place just isn't that busy. I've had a few problems with some of the hikers, but most of them are very appreciative, and they certainly are a big part of our tourist industry. It wouldn't be good for the town if they moved the trail to bypass us," explained Sophia.

"What bad experiences have you had with hikers?" I asked.

"Well, there was one woman who was just dreadful. She knocked on my door and all but demanded a room. She told me that she wasn't able to stay at The Allenberry, which in the past has always been good to hikers. She asked me how much I charged, and when I told her, she started yelling at me, telling me that wasn't the price that was quoted in her tour book. She called me a liar and told me no way would she pay that."

"Oh my God! What did you say then?" asked Julie.

"I told her that I'd had to raise my rates, and she was welcome to leave. As I was closing the door she told me there was no other place to stay close by, and she was very tired. She agreed to my price, but when I told her that she had to leave her pack outside, she resumed her tirade, telling me that was unreasonable. She said all of her belongings were in that pack, and she would be needing to get things out in the evening. I told her those were the rules and that the pack would be locked securely up in the back. She could get out what she needed. You know how awful those packs can smell. And how muddy and dirty they get. I can't be doing all of that extra cleaning anymore."

"What did she do then? Weren't you worried she might trash your place if you let her stay?" I asked.

"Well, she calmed down a little when I told her that there was a washer and dryer here, and that I would be able to wash any clothing she needed. I also decided I would call my son to come over."

"Was she OK after that?" asked Julie.

"Not exactly. When I told her there would be an additional

six dollar fee for the laundry services she got mad all over again. I explained that if she were in a motel she would be putting money in the machines and that my rate was very reasonable. She still didn't like it, and later when my son came over, she complained to him." At that point, I had a quick flash to all of the quarters we had inserted into the machines at The Clarion a couple of nights ago when we absentmindedly washed our clothes twice. We spent well over six dollars.

"He must have been upset to see his mother treated rudely. What did he say?" I asked, now very interested in the details.

Yes. I am a nosy person. My husband calls me a gossip. I call it human interest. I am a people-person. I want to know about people. Yeah. I want the dirt.

"He explained how much extra work doing the laundry is for me and then told her that if she didn't like the rules, that she should leave. He offered to help her pack up. She quieted down then."

"She didn't give you any more problems?" Julie asked.

"No. In fact, she complimented me on my breakfast the next day. I prepare a special quiche, you know. I put extra eggs and cheese in it because I know hikers are always hungry and need a good start. And later, I got a written apology from her. She explained that she was just exhausted and didn't have much money left. She said she didn't usually behave that way and hoped I wouldn't think too badly of her. I didn't. I just don't like being treated rudely. I'm in business, and I try to give my guests a good experience."

"I have to ask, is the reason you agreed to let us stay here tonight because we don't look that dirty? And we don't smell too bad?" I asked.

Sophia hesitated for just a moment, and then answered, "Well, yes. I can afford to be choosy, and it's extra work to clean the room after I've had really ripe hikers, if you know what I mean. I noticed you have a car parked outside. You aren't thru-hikers?"

"No. I'm just out here for a week, and we've done a few day

hikes and a few nights on the trail. Julie here is out for most of the summer, so this was like a break week for her. I'm a short timer," I said.

"Yeah, I have to get off the trail in a month because I start a new job. I just want to see how far I can get. My brother spent a few days with me, and now Sandy was here for the week. I'm OK by myself. This is something I've always wanted to do," explained Julie.

"Well, I do see ladies doing this alone. I certainly wouldn't want to try it. I was never much for hiking," said Sophia.

We got the gear we needed for the evening and left the rest of our stuff in Lucy. Bathing and washing out our shirts, socks and underwear was first on our agenda. Sophia showed us to our room and explained how bathroom sharing would be working. We did not object to her rules. They were certainly reasonable and nothing we couldn't live with for one night. But, let me say, this house was something else.

Our room was small. I mean, really, really small. A single bed would have fit nicely along with a dresser. I think that this was likely once used as a large, walk-in closet. And now it contained a double bed and lots of things that might well be stored in a closet. Except they weren't. They were on display. Everywhere.

Now, a double bed is cozy for a couple. In fact, at home, my husband and I share a double bed. That's nice. For us. Because we can spoon or cuddle, and neither of us cares if a stray arm or leg finds itself flung across the other. No problem. However, for two women, who are not lesbians, the double bed was not looking good. Besides, Julie snored. It was bad enough in the shelters, but then there was a symphony of snoring, so she just blended in.

Don't ask me why, but when multiple people are snoring, it doesn't seem as bothersome as when it is just one, right next to you, close enough to touch, maybe even actually touching. It is very annoying, and for someone like myself, who sleeps lightly, it is like an all night alarm clock. I would be spending my time shoving her onto her side. What if she thought that the shove was me nudging her some sort of signal? You know, to get cozy? No. This double bed wasn't looking good. And, I know Julie was thinking the same thing because she looked at the bed, and then at me, and muttered something about sleeping on the edge.

We gave ourselves a tour of the upstairs. There were dolls, lacy things, pictures, toys, games, dressers, chairs, wardrobes, all packed tightly into the other rooms and the hallway. There was really no space, either on the wall or the floor, other than the ap- proximately three foot wide space to walk. It was amazing. I could not begin to imagine the herculean task of having to clean out this place once Sophia died or moved out. I mean, my folks were depression era pack rats, but their house was vacant compared to this. We both just sort of gaped with our mouths open. You can learn a great deal about people from the things they value enough to display.

"Sandy, have you ever seen anything like it?"

"No, can't say as I have. Do you think she has ever thrown anything away?"

"It sure doesn't look like it. Hey, did you notice that our room has a sink?" asked Julie.

"No, where would a sink fit in there?"

"It's at the end of that wall of mirrors. Actually, I checked and the mirrors are closet doors. They do make the room seem bigger. I think she doesn't let people bring up their backpacks because there's no place to put them in that room," said Julie.

"Remember, we got the cheaper room because we share a bathroom. That one at the end of the hall is big enough. Even has a queen bed," I said.

"Yeah. This is good enough for one night though. We're really only here to sleep. Where do you want to eat? That same restaurant with the frazzled waitress? Or should we try the tav- ern?" asked Julie.

"Let's go to the tavern, have some wine, look at the menu and then decide. What I really want is an ice cream cone. We need to ask where we go for that," I said.

Once we were able to get past the mirrors in the room and concentrate on sorting our things, washing out our clothes, hanging them on hangers in the closet, and taking very much needed and appreciated showers, we found ourselves discussing the bathroom at great length. Neither one of us had ever, ever seen anything like it before.

It was primarily black and white. I know that might sound modern and tasteful, having sharp lines of contrast. It. Was. Not. It was likely from the seventies. The toilet, except for the seat, was black. Now, I can understand where a black toilet could totally make sense. I mean think about cleaning the bowl. How would you know if it was stained? However, if you needed to know what color your pee was, maybe for health reasons, there could be a problem. But other than that, I guess I can understand why a black toilet would be a good choice. Cleaning is made so much easier because the ring just doesn't show up. Unless it really started to stink, you were good to just leave it be.

The shower and the sinks were white with gold fixtures. The tub and shower included a large, gold stallion on hind legs. I am not sure what his purpose was meant to be other than decorative. Perhaps Sophia liked horses. Or, maybe it was a gift, and this was the only place she could think to display it. The walls that were not part of the mirror display were white with black and gold designs, sort of like flowers with ribbons stringing from them. Interesting to look at, but not something I would choose. The carpet was relatively thick and off-white. It did certainly set off the black.

There also was a wall of mirrors in the bathroom. Plus there were mirrors extending across the double sink. That was just a little unnerving because it was weird enough in the bedroom, but at least in there, we were wearing clothes. Getting out of the shower and staring at the wrinkly skin with the cellulited dimples was not exactly a boost to self esteem. I remember thinking, "Ewwww." And quickly turning away. I know that's what I look like naked, but I don't have to be reminded in such a graphic manner. Tiny bathroom mirrors are so much more flattering.

The gold trim was an interesting touch. I can't say it was exactly ugly and tacky, but it wasn't especially tasteful. Yes. Now that I think about it, ugly and tacky do sort of fit. And the gold was that sparkly stuff. You know, kind of a glittery appearance? Of course, there was the usual crocheted tissue box cover. That was also black, with gold trim. We were so intrigued with the whole scheme that we both took pictures. If ever we needed to explain a black bathroom to anyone, we had proof that it was possible. There is no accounting for taste, right? We all have our ideas about what works and what doesn't. Seeing the black bathroom showed both of us that interior design has no limits. At least the place was clean. Yes. Very clean. And, to be fair, my own house can honestly be described as Early American Rummage Sale with a touch of Salvation Army. An interior decorator would throw-up. Shit. Some of my friends and family would throw-up. And my place is certainly not as clean as Sophia's.

Although I missed being in the woods, now that I was out of the woods, I have to confess that once again experiencing amenities was nice. Strange though, all the time I was trudging through the brush with my backpack, swatting bugs, dripping sweat, and checking my pulse rate, I would be thinking about how nice it would be to get back to town, able to drive where ever I wanted to go, wash with hot water, and sleep on a mattress off the ground. But, now that I was back to where all of those things were possible, I wanted nothing more than to get back to the woods where life was simple and decisions were few. No one was around to care if you stunk, and the distractions of everyday modern life were non-existent.

Julie suggested that we have a drink at *the* tavern. I say *the* tavern, instead of *a* tavern because there was only one in town.

Boiling Springs is not a big place. I was thinking we could go back to the Italian restaurant with the frazzled waitress but wanted to have the drink first. The tavern, aptly named Boiling Springs Tavern, was a funky, rustic place. Nice. We noticed a couple other hikers bellied up to the bar like we were. How is it that we recognized them as hikers without asking? Easy. The clothes they were wearing did not quite measure up to what one might wear when going out for a drink. They wore weathered hiking boots, and they had that unkempt been-in-the-wild-a-long-time kinda look. Plus, we asked them and identified ourselves as comrades of the trail.

Actually, our clothing was also a give away. Julie had taken to wearing her newly purchased pajama bottoms from Walmart, safari hiking shirt, with her lightweight plastic *camp shoes.* OK. Flip-flops. It wasn't like just anyone could tell she was wearing pajama bottoms. I mean, it wasn't exactly Walmart-parking-lot-obvious. But, I think most women who paid the least bit of attention to public attire, would recognize the jammies. Plus, they probably had some of their own.

No, I wasn't a fashion plate, either. Of course, I never am. And in fact, really wasn't dressed much differently than I would have been at home. Gym shorts, t-shirt, safari shirt, and my own new flip-flops. Since we hadn't been on the trail that long, Julie, a little over two weeks, and me, just short of one week, we still retained a relatively coiffed appearance.

Drinking our wine, enjoying the atmosphere of the tavern and being ravenously hungry, we decided to eat there and then strike out on our quest to find ice cream. Asking for directions to the nearest place, we learned there was nothing within walking dist-ance. No problem. We had Lucy.

Have you ever noticed that as a whole, humans aren't esp-ecially adept at giving directions or estimating distances? I have. Asking two different men, we were given two sets of directions, both to the same place. Both guaranteed to be the shortest route.

Fine. We would just head out of town back toward Carlisle, and stop at the first ice cream place we saw.

Can I just say that this ice cream quest was really turning out to be some major sort of expedition? First, apparently we made a wrong turn because we somehow ended up on the interstate. I know. That is a pretty big deal wrong turn. And then, I guess we were distracted by conversation, because we missed the Carlisle exit altogether and found ourselves headed to Harrisburg. Turning around, and now plugging in the GPS, which we should have used in the beginning, or better yet, have asked our smartphones, since we had the technology to guide us. But no. We foolishly asked men for directions. I know. What were we thinking? By now we had traveled twenty miles. It was beginning to get dark. Sometimes I refer to the GPS voice as a *bitch*. The *bitch* is a good one if she manages not to get me lost. This good *bitch* took us right to Leo's Homemade Ice Cream shop, in Carlisle.

"Jule, do you remember Dave and Janice telling us about their son? The one who owned the ice cream business in Carlisle? The one where Janice takes care of all the flowers?"

"Uh, yeah, I do. Do you think this is it?"

"I do. She mentioned Leo's. And check out all of these beautiful flowers. This place isn't that big. What are the chances?"

Being the nosy girl that I am, I asked the last name of the owner. Sure enough. We were there. Small world. And I can honestly say, that Leo's homemade ice cream is totally awesome! Yes, I would get off the highway if I was driving through PA just to get a cone. Dave and Janice called us on our drive back home, offering their shuttle services once again on the following day.

This time we declined, because our plan was to drive Lucy to Scott Farm Trail ATC Crew Headquarters, where parking was available. We would leave Lucy there and get back on the trail. We did, however, ask if they could pick us up at the Hotel Doyle in Duncannon, the day after tomorrow. That would be my finish, and

I would need to get back to my car. Julie would go with me because she needed to restock her pack from all of the supplies I'd brought when I'd arrived a week ago. Wow! One week! In some ways it has seemed like I'd been out on this trail for months, and in others, no more than a minute.

We arrived back at the B & B just after dark and let ourselves in, successfully maneuvering the multiple locks. Time to hug our sides of the bed and hope we did not fall onto the floor. My side happened to be facing the mirrors. The first thing I would be looking at in the morning would be my wrinkly face with the puffy eyes and ratty hair. How attractive. Hopefully, I wouldn't frighten myself. This was the second last night of my AT adventure. Tomorrow would be a long day, roughly eleven miles to the shelter deep in the woods. The weather forecast was for more of the same. More heat, more humidity and a chance of thunderstorms.

Chapter 14: Heat, Rain, and Arrhythmia: July 13

"Jule, c'mom, we need to get down to breakfast. Sophia was pretty clear about the time, and I believe her when she says we need to be punctual."

She told us that she made a special breakfast for hikers, some kind of souffle that would hold us for most of the day. I mentioned that I didn't eat meat, so I hoped she would remember and not pack the thing with bacon and sausage. Of course, that would delight Julie, especially as she watched me either decline the thing altogether, or politely pick out the larger meat pieces, which of course, she would be more than happy to eat. I just did not understand this girl's appetite. She once downed an entire big mac and french fry order in less than five minutes while we were on a bike trip. She never told me about it until later because she was only supposed to be going into the McDonalds to use the bathroom, while I stayed outside, in the rain, watching our bikes. No. She did not bring anything out to me.

We arrived at the breakfast table, which had been nicely set on the back patio at the appointed time. We were seated promptly at 8:30 AM. Our host placed two steaming dishes of baked eggs and cheese. I have to say, she was right about this dish holding us for most of the day. I swear she used only egg yolks, heavy cream, and a pound of cheese. Tasty it was, light it was not. There was also fresh fruit with some muffins, along with our coffee, tea, and juice. I inspected the teabag to make sure it wasn't decaffeinated. I don't do coffee anymore because it gives me heartburn, but I am absolutely addicted to caffeine, and if I don't have my cup of tea by noon, I get a headache.

Caffeine headaches are the worst, aside from those resulting from an aneurysm or brain tumor. Way back when I was trying to become a more purified person and give up all chemicals and food additives (except for alcohol of course, because that is medicinal), I developed the most horrific headache. John drove me to the ER as I held my head and moaned. One CT scan later, after being bombarded with unnecessary radiation, the doc began to question me. Upon my admission of giving up caffeine three days earlier, he just dropped his pen, muttered, "Withdrawal headache," and ordered a shot of Demerol and cup of coffee for me. I wish he would have questioned me before the CT scan. Needless to say, I did not want to get a headache on my last full hiking day.

During breakfast we enjoyed a very pleasant conversation with Sophia. She told us a few more stories about pain-in-the-ass-guests. Except that she didn't use the term pain-in-the ass. That's my touch. She more appropriately said, "Difficult guests." We asked about her family. Black toilet aside, she turned out to be a classy lady.

We would be carrying full packs once again. The days spent with just food and water in our packs were certainly easier on our backs, but made our packs seem all the heavier now that we had all of our gear again. Plus, it was so very hot and humid; we each needed to carry a gallon and a half of water because the springs and streams along the trail were unreliable due to the drought. Dehydration was not something we needed to deal with at this point. I had enough trouble lugging what I had without feeling like shit from thirst.

Packing up, we loaded Lucy, said goodbye to Sophia, raved about her breakfast and drove to Sherwood Drive, about a mile past Scott Farm, to leave Lucy. Turns out the parking was safer there, and I certainly wanted Lucy safe. This would be my last full day on the trail, my last night in a shelter, my last time lugging a full pack, at least for this summer. Part of me was glad to put this adventure behind me as I now had bragging rights to the AT. Yet this teensy little voice in my head was mumbling something about doing this again, on another section of the trail, to shoot for one hundred miles of uninterrupted hiking and carrying a full pack the whole time. No slackpacking. I wasn't sure at this point. I suppose I would need to wait and see how I felt once I'd left the trail entirely. I knew that Julie planned on hiking more. She was already talking about next summer.

"Jule, I'm not feeling good about just leaving Lucy in this parking lot. She's all alone. I wonder if kids stalk this place, knowing hikers leave their cars here. I'm thinking of driving up the road and knocking on a few doors. Maybe someone will let me leave her in their driveway or their yard. I would, if someone asked me."

"Sandy, I think your car will be fine here. They told us back at that crew headquarters this was OK. People leave their cars here all the time."

"I know. But I just don't feel good. Look at her. No cars around. She looks so vulnerable."

"Sandy, it's a car."

Yeah. I know I am a little over the top with my attachment to this Subaru Forester. She is the best car I have ever owned. She's the first car I have made payments on in a long time. I spend so much time in my cars that I get kind of attached to them. Yes. I get that this is not normal behavior. Having an emotional attachment to an inanimate object is a sign of mental instability. But hey, we name ships and hurricanes, right? We refer to ships as *she.* Where did that come from? Why don't we just call hurricanes by numbers or letters? It isn't just me. The attachment and naming thing is bigger than I am. I own it. I. Love. Lucy. My car, I mean. She deserves to be taken care of and not left out in the middle of a strange parking lot.

So. I drove up the road looking for long term parking prospects. The first two doors I knocked on produced no results. There were cars parked in the driveways, but no one answered the door. The third place had a contractor's truck parked in front, and the guy was talking on his phone, as he walked around the property. I politely waited for him to hang up, and then explained my situation and request.

"Hi. I'm hiking on the Appalachian Trail for a few days and don't feel good leaving my car in that parking lot back at Sherwood Drive. I know it's supposed to be OK, but I'd feel better leaving it at a house."

I purposely avoided referring to her by name, because I didn't want the guy to think I was nuts. I do understand that most people don't name their cars and refer to them as living creatures.

"This is my last day on the trail, so it would only be until tomorrow afternoon. I'm hiking with a friend, and we have a ride lined up from Duncannon, where we'll finish."

I avoided using the term *girlfriend* because I didn't know if the guy was homophobic. He might think I was a lesbian, which would be fine, except that if for some reason he didn't like lesbians, like maybe his girlfriend had dumped him for another girl, then he might just say, "No."

I know of several men who have lost their girlfriends to other girls, and they behaved kind of strange afterward. It made them sort of bitter and resentful toward women. I'm not a man, so I don't know if it would be worse to lose out to a woman than to another man.

Girls refer to girlfriends all of the time, and they don't mean anything sexual or pertaining to an intimate relationship. They just mean friends that happen to be girls. However, I have to say, I don't know of men who refer to their close male friends as boyfriends, unless they actually have intimate relationships with them. I suppose it is just a difference with the sexes. Although I am speaking for myself regarding this issue, I suspect I am also speaking for women in general. I would much rather lose a man to another man than to a woman.

Rather than feeling like I'd lost a boyfriend or husband, I would like to think I had gained something, and also would not be suffering the lack of self esteem by questioning my attractiveness to the opposite sex. Clearly, I can't compete with a man, whereby

I do compete with other women. My experience with gay men has all been very positive. They are kind, empathetic and have excellent taste in clothing, as well as interior decorating. Maybe this is a generalization, but this is what I have seen. I know it would have been so much easier if my ex-husband had left me for a man. God knows I have always needed fashion assistance, and my taste in home décor runs a close second to my lack of clothing sense. Damn. For the past thirty years I could have been a total fashion icon and lived in a Better Homes and Garden house. Oh, how I would have preferred having a man for a wife-in-law instead of Goldilocks.

I called her Goldilocks because of the long, blonde hair. She brought nothing to the table of divorce so far as I was concerned. Oh well. Things work out. Just give them time, is what I have learned. And now, so many years have passed, that I rarely ever think of her. I no longer care.

Also, for some reason, it is socially acceptable for two women to share a bed when they are traveling, but men get all creeped out at the prospect. They would sooner sleep on the floor than crawl into bed with another man unless they are gay. I'm not sure when this concept started, because I have been reading a lot of history, and there used to be no issue with men sharing beds. It was common practice, just like with women. I guess I need to look further into that. Anyhow, I decided to not take the chance. I left out the *girlfriend* reference. For now, I just referred to hiking with a friend.

"Well, I don't see a problem. The house isn't occupied right now; the owner's having some remodeling done. But let me just check with my boss. I'll give him a quick call," said the nice contractor man.

He explained my request and permission was granted. Yes! Lucy could live at the end of the driveway until tomorrow. I felt much better about this arrangement. I had left my pack back with Julie, so I locked up Lucy and walked the roughly half a mile back to the parking lot, where she was waiting. Had I realized what was awaiting me on the trail, I certainly would not have added this extra mileage to my body.

"All set! Let's go!" I said.

Knowing that this was my last day on the trail, I tried to take more notice of the landscape. I appreciated the beauty and the tranquility of the trail, knowing I would be leaving it all behind tomorrow. It was like all of my senses were suddenly much keener, and I was on hyper alert with regard to my surroundings. My attitude and determination, at least for the first few miles, was quite exemplary. This, I am sorry to say, did not last.

The terrain was easy enough in the beginning. There were rolling hills, fields, narrow paths through thickets, and streams with water enough to soak my feet. But as the day wore on, the temperature and humidity rose. The insect repellent we were using was losing its effectiveness. The gnats were buzzing around our faces. I kept reapplying the anti-bug stuff, but I think I just sweated it off. We each started with a gallon and a half of water, which I might point out, is very heavy. Pick up a gallon of milk, then a half gallon, and strap that on your back. It's a bitch. At least, it was for me.

I knew that I would be hiking over ten miles today. According to the trail guide, it was 10.2 miles to Cove Mountain Shelter. Accounting for my trekking back from where I parked Lucy, I would be chalking up over eleven miles easily. Conversation flowed as it generally did for us. We talked about the good times of the past, our families, our divorces, remarriages, gossiped about anyone worth gossiping about, and then when we grew tired, we grew silent, and just trudged along. I have to say that I was feeling pretty spry that day. My back had not ached once for the entire time I had been hiking. This, to me, was amazing.

I don't know if it was the fact that I rarely stood in one place, or the way the pack pulled my shoulders back which straightened my spinal column, almost providing a type of traction. Whatever the reason, I was certainly glad to have this reprieve because I had experienced precious few days over the past two years without back pain. This was great! A new day! If it meant that once I returned home I would need to strap a backpack on every few days and walk a mile or two, I guess that would be my new routine. Since I was now retired, there would be no issue with pack-therapy interfering with my job.

I recall a pretty decently sized stream at about the eight mile mark. It was one of the larger ones we had come across, and there was no problem finding a deep enough place to filter and refill our water bottles. Some streams were pretty skimpy, and it was a good practice to always find a spot where you could actually see the water flowing, even if it was slow. Stagnant water, even with a filter, isn't the best idea. Sometimes hikers have to resort to using it, but it's always best to avoid it if at all possible. This stream was not only flowing well, but it was over a foot deep in some places, and was perfect for soaking my very hot and tired feet.

Needless to say, off came my shirt, and into the stream it went. I didn't even bother wringing it out because I was so hot, the cold water felt great. Of course, I poured the cold water over my head and was so very thankful that there were no mirrors on the trail. Attractive, I was not. Care about my appearance? I did not. I wished there was a shelter at this stream because it would have been the perfect place to stay.

But there was no shelter, no place to camp and we needed to push on to Cove Mountain. As I was putting my socks and shoes back on, another hiker approached. I did a double take at how fast he was moving. He wasn't exactly jogging, but pretty close. His pack was enormous, as were many of the ones we saw, and he looked to be in his mid forties. He told us he already hiked about seventeen miles that day. How nice. We did not mention our puny eight. He also told us about his goal of finishing the entire trail in some amazingly short period of time. Fine for him. I looked up at the very steep hill. I would call it a mountain, but realistically, it was just a hill, and watched him all but run up the thing. He looked like a mountain goat. We were not goats. At least, I was not. Julie, maybe a little.

Actually, it was here that in hindsight, I made a big mistake. I should have eaten something. My problem with heat and exertion is that it totally kills my appetite. Since I know this, it would seem I would be smart enough to force myself to eat so that I wouldn't start to feel puny. By puny, I mean kind of weak, lightheaded. Just not good. But no. I drank plenty of water and watched as Julie ate some of her snacks. And, to her credit, she did remind me that I probably needed some more calories. And to my not credit, or stupidity, I declined.

"No thanks. I'm not hungry. I'll grab something in a while. Will you look at those fucking rocks and how steep that mountain is?"

"Yeah, I know. I like it better with the switchbacks. Let's get going. It looks like it could rain. I heard something about thunderstorms later today," said Julie.

So. Up. Up. Up we climbed. It was one of the longer and steeper climbs I had done, and I needed to stop and rest a couple of times. I always liked when it was Julie who suggested we rest. I felt less wimpy. I would tell myself I needed to go slower and rest more because I was older. Hey, two years is two years, and the older you get, the more significant a year can be. She was just entering her sixties. I was well on my way up the chronological ladder. My rungs were getting a little wobbly.

It was at about the ninth mile that I started to feel not very well. I noticed, without checking my pulse, that it wasn't exactly regular. I was skipping beats, having extra beats, and was generally tachycardic. I didn't feel like I was going to pass out, but I was really tired. It was at this point that the thunder began. I was walking behind Julie and didn't want to ask her to stop yet again, because I realized getting to the shelter before the thunderstorm hit would be a very good idea. I fumbled around in my belly bag and pulled out a protein bar, unwrapped it hurriedly, and stuffed it in my mouth. It was a little tough choking it down as I walked along with no water, but I managed, telling myself this was all I needed to feel OK.

It. Did. Not. Work. I did not feel better. Now, realizing just how deep into the woods we were and how likely it would be for help to arrive should I actually suffer a heart attack right here, I experienced a moment of shear terror. Shit. Fuck. Damn. What if I died out here? Plopped right down in the middle of the trail. Julie wouldn't even know right away because she was ahead of me. It was now raining. It was raining pretty hard, and the thunderclaps were getting closer together. Lightning flashed all around us, and I was thinking about my funeral.

I wondered if they would be sending a helicopter to retrieve my body and then realized that would not be possible because there was no place for it to land. Much like a ski slope rescue, the paramedics would need to carry a stretcher up the mountain. I was sure I wouldn't be the first to die on the trail, but that didn't make me feel any better. I thought of telling Julie that I wasn't doing well but then decided against it. Better to just keep walking as long as I could, and hope for the best. Once we reached the shelter I could lay down and just die there. Other hikers would be around to help Julie. Maybe I could even summon up the strength for some final words.

My pulse was really erratic now. I wasn't sure why I wasn't feeling worse than I was. Being the good nurse, I was constantly assessing myself. Dizzy? No. Weak? Sort of, but not weak enough to not be able to carry my pack and put one foot in front of the other. Could I think clearly? Yes. That was a good sign. I was just very, very tired. I told myself that the arrhythmia was benign, and the result of low electrolytes. That did not take away my growing anxiety, because I knew that if electrolytes became too off balance, it could kill you. Low potassium can stop a heart. Nice. This knowledge was not helping. Shit. That protein bar had to be of some benefit. Maybe there was just enough potassium in the thing to keep me alive, at least for another hour or so. Now, the rain was really pelting us. No, we had not stopped to put on rain gear or cover our packs. That was really pretty stupid of us. Having dry clothing and sleeping bag was sort of important. Too late for that. Our bags probably couldn't get any wetter.

With every step I took, I told myself, "Just a few more feet and you will be at the shelter." This was very misleading self-talk.

Meeting up with a couple other hikers who seemed to know more about the trail than we did, we asked them if they knew how far it was to the Cove Mountain Shelter.

"Probably about a mile. We're not stopping tho. It's only another five miles into Duncannon so we're going to head there for the night. We want to stay at The Doyle."

More talk of The Doyle. Even in my less than stellar condition, I was wanting to see this place. I still had not told Julie how crappy I was feeling, so I just plodded on behind her, not needing to check my pulse for extra beats, because I could feel them. I remember just being thankful I was able to remain upright. On we walked. On I plodded. At some point, the rain stopped briefly, and a rainbow in the woods was visible. Julie stopped and pointed it out to me. I wish I could have been more excited, but all I could think of was the shelter, the bunk I would collapse onto, and how stupid I had been for not eating more during the day. I recall faking interest in the rainbow, which really was a remarkable thing, but I just didn't have the enthusiasm to actually appreciate this wonder of nature. I was too busy wondering if I would remain alive long enough to eat dinner that night.

Interesting, although I gave a great deal of thought to my impending rescue, I really was not overly anxious about my situation. I knew I couldn't stop walking, because there was absolutely no place we could have camped, even if we wanted. The trail was very narrow, with thick brush and woods on either side. If we stopped, there was no place to put up a tent or shelter and no way we could start a fire. It wouldn't take long before we became chilled and hypothermic. No, we needed to keep moving. There was no point in my complaining, because there was nothing to do but get to the shelter. If I should drop dead, Julie would soon figure out I wasn't behind her and go back to find me. At that point, whatever she chose to do would no longer matter, because I would be dead. My corpse would present some issues, but there would be no rush to get me out of there. I mean, it would be a day or two before I would start to swell and stink. By then, I would certainly have been removed.

Stop it!! I had to stop thinking like this. It was not healthy. Not productive. And, I was even creeping myself out. No! I needed to think positive! We would make it to the shelter, and I would drink more water and eat some salty food. I would rest. I would get out of my wet clothes and into my hopefully dry sleeping bag.

Even though I was no longer sweating, since the rain took care of my issue with overheating, this was proving to be the hardest mile of the hike for me. Thankfully, the terrain was relatively level. I doubt I could have climbed a hill. And lived. Well, maybe I would have lived, but I am pretty sure I would have passed out at some point. We had been silent for awhile now. I don't know how Julie was feeling, but I don't think she had sunk to the physiologic abyss I was currently dwelling in. I suspect that she was getting tired, but would have been able to walk on as far as was necessary.

The protein bar I had eaten awhile ago had done nothing for me. I felt no better, no worse. However, now I could run my tongue over the nuts and pieces of cereal that were stuck between my teeth. I suppose that was a good sign. The fact that I was concerned with tooth debris told me that I wasn't ready to check out yet. There was some pride remaining in my very exhausted, heart-beat-skipping body.

The sign that read Cove Mountain Shelter, .1 miles, with a

downward pointing arrow, was absolutely, without a doubt, over-whelmingly, the most welcoming sign I have ever seen, on or off the trail. One tenth of a mile was nothing! It was like a city block. We should actually see the shelter from our turn off the trail. Except we did not. I don't know who measures these distances and what instrument is used, but this one tenth of a mile was one very, very, very long stretch. It wasn't just that I felt like shit. It just kept winding down, down, around, and down some more. I kept thinking that should I survive the night, I might not be able to carry my pack back out to the main trail in the morning.

"Jule, is it just me, or is this seeming like a long way down?"

"It's a long way down. Maybe they marked the sign wrong. Or, maybe we're just really tired."

Finally arriving at the small shelter, definitely the smallest one of the three I had seen, we were greeted by four hikers already hunkered down for the rainy night. Yes. It was still raining. Their gear was already spread out on the bunks, but I was feeling so pitiful, I just laid down on one of them, and meekly asked if who-ever had claimed it, minded if I rested there for awhile, telling him I wasn't feeling very well.

The shelter inhabitants were all young guys, likely in their twenties, and they could not have been kinder. I think they looked at us and saw their mothers. Or, looking at my gray hair, maybe grandmother.

"No problem, m'am. You just keep the bunk. I'm fine on the floor. Are you hungry? Do you want some of my mac and cheese? I've got beef jerky here, too. Really, I've got plenty," offered one very, kind young man.

"No thanks, I'm OK. We have food. I just need to lay here for a few minutes."

"Sandy, you need some calories. Eat something while I go and get our water."

I followed her orders, like an obedient child and did not offer to help with the water filtering. Yes. I was pathetic. And I don't think I could have walked the additional one tenth of a mile to the stream, if my life depended on it. The way I was feeling, it likely would, because the arrhythmia had not subsided.

After eating a dry, stale, buttered roll, I felt slightly, and I do mean slightly, better. I was starting to get cold. I would have to get these wet clothes off and into my *camp clothes*, which consisted of the black tights and safari shirt I slept in at night. Since it was still raining and the privy was about fifty yards back behind the shelter, the only way I would be able to put on my dry clothing would be to do it right there, in the shelter, with the four young men, who were chatting about their day, and eating their mac and cheese and beef jerky. What the hell. I was cold. These things had to come off.

So. Right there at the back of Cove Mountain Shelter, I stripped naked, put on my dry clothes, wrung out and hung up the wet ones, and I can honestly say, it was a total non-event. You know how you can sense when someone is looking out of the corner of their eye? They don't want you to know they are looking, but just can't resist sneaking a peek? Well, I can honestly say, there was no peek sneaking going on there. These guys could not have been more uninterested in the granny lady stripping. I was not even remotely on their chick-radar. Perhaps because somewhere along the way, I had grown from a chick to a hen.

Who wants to look at a hen? Well, maybe a horny old rooster would be interested, These young men were certainly not horny old roosters. Actually, there comes a time when clothing is such a very wonderful blessing. So very many sins are hidden under clothing. I know that sometimes when I am at boring meetings, I have this way of passing time, in addition to doodling, where I try and picture everyone in the room naked. Generally speaking, it is not an attractive visualization. Most times, it's downright scary. Actually terrifying. So, I am pretty sure that these young men were into the self-preservation mode, sparing themselves from a future of playing the mental movie of the old gray mare hiker in the flesh. If I was in my twenties, I wouldn't be peeking at a sixty-something man with sagging skin. Not only would I not peek, I would avoid the visual confrontation at all costs. Smart young men in this shelter. I have seen myself in the mirror. No one needs to have nightmares in an AT shelter. Worrying about an intruding bear, a skunk, a rabid coon, that is plenty to be concerned about. Adding an older naked lady to the list is just not helpful.

My wet clothes off, dry ones on, at least I wasn't cold anymore. Still I wasn't feeling well. Julie returned with our water and cooked our dinner. Cooking freeze dried food isn't especially tough, but still, it does require some effort. I was grateful that Julie was feeling well enough to get our water and make dinner. I was just plain wasted. I did feel encouraged, however, after eating. The arrhythmia was much less noticeable. Checking my pulse indicated much longer periods of a normal sinus pattern, and I was feeling a little better. Looking back, I suspect that my potassium and sodium were both too low, caused from excessive perspiring and lack of appropriate calories. If ever I did this again, there would be one water bottle full of an electrolyte solution. I would not feel this way again by choice or lack of preparation.

I mentioned earlier that my need to pee in the night was somehow directly proportional to the inconvenience it presented. Resting on the bunk at the back of the shelter, while outside the rain continued to fall lightly, but steadily, produced an unusual amount of urinary urgency. Five times I fumbled for my headband with the small light in the front and made my way out of the shelter, out to the back. I should have walked up to the privy. I did not. Too far. Too dark. Too likely I might trip and splat. Too likely I would come face to face with some nocturnal creature of the forest. I loved the creatures way, way more when I was tucked securely in my sleeping bag, at the back of the shelter.

I don't know if this was some sort of physiological response to how exhausted I had felt last night, but I do know after expelling a considerable amount of urine in the night, I felt totally normal in

171

the morning. No irregular pulse, no tiredness. I was ready to hike. I was even ready to hike up the beastly hill that was supposedly only one tenth of a mile. Bring it on! My pack and I were ready for the day. I suppose that the knowledge of only a four mile hike didn't hurt my spirits any. Plus, after climbing out of the area the shelter rested in, our hike was all downhill, into the city of Dun-cannon. Our adventure was winding down. Amazing how quickly time had passed since the day I pulled into Caledonia State Park, excited almost beyond words to begin my first hike on the Appal-achian Trail.

Chapter 15: The Doyle and the End: July 14

As the sun rose and daylight streamed into our crowded little home deep in the mountains of Pennsylvania, it became quickly apparent just how crowded we had become. The shelter had four bunks and could reasonably accommodate four more average sized persons on the floor. Counting heads, I came up with twelve. I am not sure how they all fit as several had now rolled up their sleeping bags and were packing up their gear. But, apparently they did. Julie told me it was just an unspoken rule of the trail, that you always made room in a shelter, no matter how crowded it got. This was especially true if the weather was bad. No one was ever turned out and made to sleep in a storm. At least that's what she had noticed, and it seemed to hold true. Granted, it would be possible to pitch a tent in a storm, just not something you looked for the opportunity to do.

For the last time, perhaps forever for me, unless I dragged my ass back up to another section of the AT for another adventure, I ate my breakfast as I sat perched at the front of the shelter dangling my legs off the edge. I had to be careful where I sat because there was a very thin metal sheet nailed to the edge, and it would be easy to slice a hand, a leg, a foot, or any part of your body that carelessly scraped across it. I mentioned this to a couple of the other hikers, and they told me it was because there had been a large possum infestation, and this was a way to keep them out of the shelters. Hmmm. I suppose arriving in a shelter late at night, in a rainstorm, only to be greeted with beady little eyes staring out from the corners could be a little unnerving. They would likely be as wary of us as we would be of them and perhaps not really be especially welcoming.

I also found an explanation of the possum problem in the shelter's guest log. It is customary for all hikers to sign the guest logs in each of the shelters using not their real names, but the trail name they acquired. I guess it is supposed to give a general idea about the number of hikers that utilize the trail and shelters each year. Before the age of cell phones, it was a way to track hikers should a problem arise and someone need to contact them in an emergency. I signed my real name to the logs, because I had not been on the trail long enough to get a trail name. It was the thru-hikers, and the longer section hikers, like Julie, who would get the trail names.

We were the last of the dozen campers to leave the shelter that morning, hitting the trail at about 8:30 AM. I could tell it was going to be another scorcher of a day, and already the humidity was settling in. I didn't mind putting on my still wet clothes. It actually felt good. What did it really matter anyway? My shirt would be soaking wet again if I came to a stream, as would my hair, because I would dip both. My pants were made of that lightweight, breathable material that dries quickly. I did have dry underwear. As expected, I had no problem hiking up the hill to get back on the trail. Knowing it was going to be such a short hike energized me. Perhaps I am meant to be an under ten mile a day hiker. Downhill is my friend. We all find our grooves; I am thinking that is mine.

I remember back on the second or third day one of the young girls we met along the trail reported that for the first few weeks, eight miles seemed to be her limit. Gradually, she increased her stamina, and when we spoke with her, she found nothing particularly challenging about a twenty mile hike. I suppose that it is all relative to what a person is used to doing. Back when I was running marathons, a six mile run was nothing. It almost seemed like I hadn't even run at all. Today? Six miles of running? All I can say, is it would not be happening. Before this hike a four mile walk was a big day!

Gear stowed away, packs donned, we set off on the path up the hill that would lead us back to the AT. Yes! It was a beautiful day! It could have been raining and hailing; it still would have been beautiful. I was completing my eighth day hiking on the Appalachian Trail, my back did not ache, and I was in a normal sinus rhythm. What more could a girl ask for? Julie and I chatted as we wound our way through the woods and down the steep embankments. I was starting to look ahead, getting out of the moment and planning what I would be doing for the first few days after returning to *civilized life.*

Although my time in the woods had been brief, it really impacted me. Physically, I found it way more way difficult than running a marathon. Emotionally, I found it to be an enrichment beyond words. It gave me the opportunity to disconnect from life's everyday distractions, to reflect on the choices I made over the years that had brought me to this moment, to this mountain, and to accept that I did the best I could do, given what I had known. I had succeeded in the climb. How many more chances would I have? I would like to think there will be many more opportunities to "hike." And each one will be embraced.

About two miles into the day's hike, which was actually just about half way, we stopped for a photo op on top of a huge boulder that overlooked the entire Susquehanna River Valley. The view was breathtaking, and the fact that it was a sunny, clear day made it that much more magnificent. I was remembering another mountain that Julie and I were on top of some sixteen years ago in Vermont, when we biked up Hogback and took in the one hundred mile view.

We were different women then, in our mid forties, and still thinking we could figure out life. I had just gotten married for the second time; Julie had just gotten divorced for the first time, from her high school boyfriend. Granted, sometimes those very young marriages can and do work out, but Julie and I were poster girls for those that did not. There was yet another mountain on the Gaspe Peninsula, the one with the seventeen percent grade, where we not only pushed our bikes up, but also down. Julie had just met the man who would become her second husband, and I was committed to having a successful marriage with my second husband, John. We were still in our forties, but certainly a good bit more emotionally weathered. We were becoming seasoned babes, improving with age in the areas that really mattered. We were becoming the fine wine and cheese of women.

I don't know if I should read some sort of prophetic symbolism in our trips to the tops of mountains. Each time we took pictures, as we did this morning. Each time I see these pictures, side by side, I think of what it took to get me to the place the photo was taken. The one of me on this boulder is now my favorite picture of myself and is my new Facebook profile. I like it because it makes me look like I know what I am doing with a backpack strapped on and a pair of hiking poles. I like it because it reminds me of where I am in my life, and although I am not young anymore, at least physically, neither am I old. I'm at a good place. Since it is taken at a distance, none of my wrinkles show! I look good! I look like I am not almost sixty-two! I love it!

While we were resting on the boulder, several other hikers came by. One, Jim, stopped to talk with us. He was a day hiker, which is always apparent from the size of one's pack. Folks are just wearing regular backpacks, not the full-sized ones crammed full with bottles and shoes draping off them. Jim was easy to talk with, mentioning his wife, which immediately took him off the table for Julie's dating considerations. It wasn't like she was looking for prospects, but if she were at a different point in her life, and maybe thought about it once again, which right now she swears she never will, the presence of a spouse is an immediate deal-breaker. At least, it is for us. Plus, he was a little on the young side. Since when was fifty young? Well, if you are a sixty year old woman, it is very young. Except for cougars. A ten year span is totally OK for them, and it is totally fine to be a cougar.

We talked briefly about hiking, and somewhere in the conversation organ donation weaved its way into the subject matter.

Jim mentioned, very casually, that three years ago he donated a kidney to his best friend. Wow! That is not the offhand remark you expect to hear. First of all, what are the chances that you would actually be a perfect organ match for your best friend? And secondly, even if you were, that is one very large commitment to make. I am not saying I wouldn't do it. It's just that somewhere in the back of your mind lurks the possibility that maybe your child would need a kidney. Julie and I had a mutual friend who had done just that, donated a kidney to her daughter. Sadly, her daughter's body rejected the kidney.

Obviously, we don't need two kidneys to live, but if we have given one away, then we no longer have that option. I don't know. That is a tough one. Right now, because my child is healthy, and my kidneys are fine so far as I know, I would like to think that if someone I knew needed one, I would step up for the big hit. I think of them as sort of a surplus account. It's like when you have extra money in the bank, and you keep it just in case, but you hope that you don't need to tap the account. However, I have learned, what we think we would do, and how we actually respond are sometimes not the same. I am going to assume I would give the kidney. I would break into my account. I like myself better when I think that way.

Jim told us about the surgery and how the first thing that both he and his friend did together once they were out of the hospital was to take a hike. I thought that was amazing. And pretty cool. We sat on the boulder with him for about half an hour, learned about other big hikes he had taken, and his new brewery business. We parted ways, and as he continued up the hill, we headed down.

With every step I took down, I reminded myself how tough this part of the trail would be to travel in reverse. I would not want to be climbing up these steep rock steps. I was also very thankful that it was not raining today, because slipping on this part of the trail could be a very painful, if not deadly, experience. I just put one foot in front of the other, planted my poles, and continued down the path.

Arriving in the borough of Duncannon, which is actually a part of the Harrisburg-Carlisle metropolitan area was a bit of a letdown. I think because although I knew that I would only be spending a short time on the trail, I tried very hard to live in the moments. I didn't look ahead, until yesterday. Knowing that my micro-adventure was nearing an end, I did start to make my mental *to do* lists. Seeing the city limits sign was like opening the last present on Christmas morning. You want to see what's in the present, but you don't want the celebration to be over.

"Jule, we're here! I actually did it! I hiked on the Appalachian Trail and my back still doesn't hurt!"

"Yes, you did! I'm so glad our week went the way it did! Every part of it was good. It was all meant to be."

Of course, she didn't know just how shitty I felt last night, how near to death I thought I was, and frankly, decided that was information she just didn't need. Bad enough I started out on my stint of the hike whining incessantly about how steep the hills were. She didn't need to know the morbid twist I had inserted near the end. And the end was approaching fast. We were moving right along.

Finding the blazes in town, painted on telephone poles, seemed a little odd. I became so accustomed to seeing them in the woods, marking trees and rocks, they just didn't seem to belong on city streets, looking at cars whizzing by. In fact, we missed a couple of them and had to do a brief turn around. Checking the trail guide for what would be my final time, we found our destination, The Doyle.

The Doyle is an early nineteenth century four story hotel. The address is 7 North Market Street, and it is a sight not easily, or likely ever, forgotten. The original structure was three stories high, built in the 1770's out of wood, and was a most welcome refuge to travelers. It was, and notice the past tense, an elegant piece of architecture, boasting of such guests as Charles Dickens.

Sadly, this local landmark burned but was rebuilt in the early 1900's. Passing through the hands of several owners, it came up for sale in 2001 and was purchased by Pat and Vickey Kelly.

Although it was known as a place for hikers to stay over the years, a policy had been put into place whereby *dirty hikers* were not welcome. Well. Let me tell you something about *dirty hikers*. If one has spent at least one night in a shelter or tent on the Appalachian Trail, one is likely dirty. If it has rained and there is a significant amount of mud, which, of course after a rain, there is, one is dirty. If several nights on the trail have occurred, one is really dirty and by now, stinking. It just is not possible to be well groomed while spending an extended period of time in the woods. So, near as I can figure, the only hikers that would have been welcomed at The Doyle would have been those day hikers out for a stroll. It had only been two days since Julie and I showered, and we already stunk. Before Pat and Vickey got here our lack of hygiene would have forced us on past this amazingly memorable place.

The AT guide describes it as "cheap," boasting of rooms from twenty-five dollars with an additional ten dollars per person in the less than spacious rooms. Coming off the trail, after sleeping on the ground in a wet tent, smelling so foul that it's difficult to even tolerate your own odor, having water actually spew forth at the turn of a nozzle and not having to bury your poo in a hole, is nothing short of luxury. If you could see The Doyle, you would gasp that I use the word luxury in the same sentence. However, in contrast to carrying all of your belongings on your back for days, weeks, months at a time, and suddenly having all of the conveniences offered up by The Doyle, well, that is truly luxury. Plus, there is also some tradition, like a right of passage, for hikers to stay there. I have to admit, I was just a little sad to be missing out on this experience. I didn't, however, feel badly enough to postpone my homecoming another day to stay there. Julie would be having that experience, and she could tell me about it. I could live vicariously through her on this one and not really mind. I was OK with not sleeping there.

The stately old place was easy to spot from a distance. Although we had not seen a picture of it beforehand, there was no doubt what we were heading toward. It looked funky from afar. From close up? Well, the term fire hazard did come to mind. However, I am sure that there would be all sorts of codes the owners would need to comply with, even if this wasn't New York State. For those readers who don't live in New York, although we certainly have a great deal to offer with regard to forests, mountains, finger lakes, great lakes, rivers, canals, wines, biking and hiking trails, we also maintain a very long list of regulations. If New York State is nothing else, it is well regulated. Our tax dollars are always hard at work. Even if we don't especially like the jobs they are working at.

"Jule, check this place out. Have you ever seen anything like it?"

"No, can't say I have. Let's belly up to the bar and have a drink."

"You want a beer this early?"

"No, I was thinking a coke. Or maybe iced tea. Hey, you're good at talking to people. When we get in there, see what you can do to get me one of the better rooms," said Julie.

"Do you really think there's much difference in room quality?"

"Maybe not. But I want one with a window. Near the bathroom would be good, too."

Walking into the grand old Doyle we found the bar to be remarkably quaint. The room was clean, and the only request the bartender made of us was to leave our packs either outdoors or in the entryway. That seemed fair. I could see how the bar might get cluttered up quickly if all the hikers propped their packs up in the corners or at the tables. There were three large packs already on the floor. I know I shouldn't have done it, but I lifted one of them up. I wanted to see just how heavy it was because the monstrosity was at least twice the size of mine.

"OMG! This thing must weigh at least seventy-five pounds! How can these guys carry all this shit?"

"Well, they're probably thru-hikers, they're a lot bigger than we are, and they're probably used to it. I know that after a week, I was doing OK with my pack, and that had to be like thirty-five pounds. When I started, I couldn't even swing it up on my back. My brother, Bruce, had to put it on me."

Before going into the bar, I checked myself out in the ladies room, as well as checking out the conditions in there. That would tell me volumes about what Julie could expect with her room. Besides, I had to pee. Not bad. Clean enough. I wouldn't want to eat off the floor, but then I wouldn't need to be worrying about that prospect. Julie was already sitting at the bar when I walked into the room.

The bartender was busy as there were several other hikers sitting at various tables. Some stunk, some did not. One guy was wearing only his rain gear. Guess his other clothes were in the laundry. It isn't like hikers carry a wide assortment of things to wear. The perverted part of me deduced that he probably didn't have underwear on under that plastic stuff and how uncomfortable that had to feel. Why I think of these things, I do not know. I was in no way thinking sexual thoughts about this very young boy, only how stiff such material would feel against sensitive tissues. It made me shudder to consider myself in a similar get-up. I didn't mention my ponderings to Julie. Maybe she was thinking the same thing. Or, maybe it would creep her out. Silence seemed like the best option here.

"Hi, I'm Sandy, and this is Julie. I'm a short timer on the trail. I've been out eight days and am heading home. Julie's out for another month. This is quite the place here. Are you the owner?"

"Yup. That's me. Me and my husband own it. I'm Vickey.

Are either of you ladies stayin' here tonight?"

"I'd like to. I've heard a lot about it. Everyone I've talked with on the trail says I need to stay here," answered Julie.

"Well, what you see is what you get. Ain't nothin' fancy. The place is old, the rooms are rough. But it's a bed and a bath. Better than sleepin' on the ground is what the hikers tell me. Twenty-nine dollars a night with tax. Another ten if your friend wants to share your room."

"OK. It will just be me. Can I have a room with a window? And is there a bathroom in it?" asked Julie.

"Honey, all the rooms got windows. You'd suffocate from the heat if they didn't. Even got a fan. The bathrooms are all shared. Yours'll be right next door. You want to see it now?"

"No, we'll have our drinks first. Can I have a root beer? Sandy, you want one, too?"

"That sounds good," I said, only too happy to extend my adventure just a little longer.

"Is there a place to do laundry around here? Within walking distance?" asked Julie.

"Right across the street. All the hikers stayin' here use the place," said Vickey.

We chatted briefly with another couple of hikers. They were all thru-hikers, intent on getting to Maine before mid October, which is when Mt. Katahdin closed its trails for the winter. Being on the mountain after that was considered too dangerous, so the thru-hikers were really on a time schedule. They knew how many miles a day they needed to average if they were to complete the AT in one season. Julie mentioned wanting to eventually hike the entire trail, in sections, over vacations and summers for the next few years. I harbored absolutely zero desire to add this to my bucket, or fuckit list, whichever term fits.

I was now sure I had at least one more section in me, maybe another week or two, but that would likely be enough for me. At least that was what I was thinking today, July 14th, 2016, just six weeks short of my sixty-second birthday. Maybe I would change my mind. But, I didn't think so. There were too many other things I wanted to do. And, as I often reminded Julie, I was way more dolphin than mountain goat. I loved the water. I was a good swimmer and wanted to cross some Finger Lakes. That was my current quest. Along with improving my bagpipe and banjo skills. And maybe completing a few more pallet projects. I had yet to hit my mark as a bonafide retired person in that I only had a couple of weeks to my credit. I would be doing something more significant than honing my less than mediocre musical skills and doing some crafts. I would figure it out. For now, this hike was sure a great way to kick it off.

Finishing our drinks, we were becoming time conscious. I did want to get home today, and I was looking at a four to five hour drive depending upon the flow of traffic and the weight of my foot on the accelerator. We still needed to get back to where I parked my car on Sherwood Drive. Julie would repack her gear, after thinning out those things she didn't need, and adding those additional items she had asked me to bring when I met up with her last week in Caledonia State Park. I wanted to shower and change my clothes before returning to *civilization.* My choices for a shower would be at The Doyle or back in Boiling Springs at the public swimming pool.

We called Dave and Janice, telling them where we were. They agreed to shuttle us one last time, and it was going to take them about forty five minutes to get down here. I was so glad that I had had that slate sketching in the car to give them. Their generosity had been beyond anything we could ever have expected.

"Jule, let's check out your digs for the night. I'm curious about what this place looks like upstairs."

"Vickey, could you show me my room for the night?" asked Julie.

"Sure can. Remember. This place is old. It ain't perfect. We do the best we can to keep the price down for the hikers," said

Vickey.

We climbed up several flights of stairs, and I noticed the beautiful woodwork displayed by the moldings and the banisters. Often times wood of this vintage was painted over. Clearly, no one had ever taken the time to do that in The Doyle, and the result was the original finish on the wood. That said, Vickey was dead-on right about the place not being perfect. It. Was. Not. The room assigned to Julie was small, with a twin bed, torn sheets, no blanket (which considering how hot and sticky it was did make a certain amount of sense), a small table, and as Vickey had promised, a window with a fan. That was the room. It was relatively clean. I mean, there were no apparent dirt piles on the floor. The sheets, although very, very, very well worn and harboring multiple holes, one of which was large enough for my hand to go through, also looked clean.

Then, there was the bathroom. Oh. My. Saying it was in rough shape is being quite subtle. And, very kind. There were such dark stains in the toilet, on the toilet, in and around the shower, and on the floor, that it was difficult to ascertain just what color these amenities were supposed to be. I can't really say with accuracy that the place was dirty, because there was no odor. So, maybe it really was sanitary enough, and the fact that it was just so very old prevented the appearance of actually being clean. Let me just say, however, that I quickly made up my mind to shower at the public pool in Boiling Springs. If that wasn't open for some reason, I planned to look for a creek. Or even a large mud puddle. I was not going to step into that shower. Uh uh. Put me back on the trail, and let me stink.

I found it an amazing contrast between the condition of the place beyond the first floor. The bar and restaurant area was fine. Clean. Decent. Julie's room for the night and her shared bathroom? Not so much. I would rather have emptied a chamber pot. Finishing our tour of the suite, I suppose one could call a room with a bathroom just around the corner a suite, we went back downstairs and outside to wait for Dave and Janice.

Duncannon is clearly a blue collar town. It has a population of roughly fifteen hundred people and was actually famous for building Lightning Glider sleds from 1904–1988. In fact, it was credited for manufacturing more children's sleds than any other factory in the US back in 1920. Incidentally, that was the year women won the right to vote, and my dad was born. Sometimes I find it hard to believe that we had only been voting for thirty-four years before I was born and that my dad is dead. Women's suffrage and death aside, Duncannon was apparently the "sled-making-capital" of the US. But now, like so many towns and cities, the jobs have been shipped overseas, and the local plants have closed. Duncannon had that feel of having once been a thriving community and was now just hanging on. The fact that the AT ran along North High Street through the center of town was important for local mer-chants, providing business for the local laundromat and small grocery stores from the hikers.

At one time Duncannon served as an important hub for both land and water travel, being located on the river and having the railroad, which was the main line to the west, open in 1849. There were originally two tracks running thru the center of town. This is now referred to as the Apple Tree Alley Walk Corridor. Also, the oldest structure remaining in the town is the Clark's Ferry Tavern. This served as the landing of Clark's Ferry, a tavern, stage stop and Inn, post office, and in the 1860's, a civil war recruiting office.

Julie and I had no time for sight seeing that day. We spent the limited amount of time we did have waiting in front of The Doyle, taking pictures, marveling at the old structure, and trying to put into words, as best we could, a summary of the past eight days. This was difficult to do, because although the time was limited, we did manage to pack a variety of experiences into it. We would definitely have some tales to tell to those friends and family who were interested in hearing about our mini-adventure. Certainly we made some great memories for the *home*, should the time come when we might need to rerun the films in our minds. Hopefully they would remain sharp enough to recall.

Dave was timely with his arrival and for yet one final time, tossed our bags into the back of his pristine pickup. Janice had begged off, Dave told us, because she had a lot of loose ends she needed to catch up. I know this couple had certainly given a good deal of their free time to shuttling us around for the past few days, along with their gas. Once again, I was thankful for the slate etching I had been able to leave for them.

"Wow! That's quite the place. I've heard about it, but never seen it this close up before," said Dave, motioning to The Doyle, as he pulled away.

"You really need to see the inside to appreciate it. Actually, what you need to see is one of the rooms up over the bar. The bar is decent. Clean and kind of funky. It's kind of hard to describe the rooms for rent," I said.

"Yeah. This is my house for the night. I'm all checked in. Hikers say that part of the experience is to eat and stay at The Doyle. So, I'm getting the full experience," said Julie.

"Are you sure you want to do that? You know, Janice and I don't have any plans. You would be more than welcome to stay with us in the cabin for tonight. Really. It's no problem. We would love to have you."

I waited for Julie to respond because this was her night. I would be back in my own cozy little double bed tucked in with my hubby deep in the woods in our little cabin type house. I would not have minded spending one more night, but my preference was to point Lucy north and head for home. I knew John would be close to his limit of kitty litter box patrol and cooking for himself. He was confined to quarters because of my two precious pussycats, unable to even venture out to visit his children, who would have been more than happy to house and feed him.

"Thanks so much. We really appreciate your offer, but I want to stay here, and I know Sandy needs to get home," said Julie.

"Yes, thanks so much. I do need to get back. We really, really want you and Janice to come up and visit us! John and I have a guest room, and I know Julie's got room in her guest apartment. We could visit a couple of wineries. So, you need to just plug a trip to Corning into your planner," I said.

"Well, if you're sure. Janice and I would love to visit. After our vacation later this summer, we can make some plans."

We described the interior of The Doyle, especially the décor of Julie's room to Dave on the drive back to where Lucy was parked. But already, I was disconnecting from *the moment*, and my mind was racing ahead, crammed with the very long and completely unnecessary to-do list I had conjured up for myself. As I mentioned previously, there have only been a couple of times in my adult life when I have allowed myself to be completely in the moment. It is not a virtue I am proud of, and it is one of the things that I would most like to change about myself. But, as we all know, the older we get, the more difficult change becomes. Still, it is possible. This is a growth area for me. And, at least for most of the past week, I did experience life in the moment. I just need to keep reminding myself about how good it felt.

My husband keeps reminding me of this fault of mine. He, more than any person I have ever met, manages to live his life that way, pretty much all of the time. The old saying that refers to the past as being gone, the future uncertain, but the present being truly a present, to be appreciated by us, totally applies to him. This is certainly good in so many ways, but not so practical in others. I think the key is a balance between the moment and planning ahead.

The best example I can think of is the story of The Three Little Pigs. John is most definitely the straw house piggy, and I am the one who lugged the bricks. He enjoys his life to the max and weathers the storms with a smile and a manner that allows him to always talk his way into the brick house, metaphorically speaking. I operate in the zone of always preparing for the storm, and I miss a lot of the sunny days. The ideal would be for John to haul a few more bricks and for me to look for the good in the straw house. Sometimes we manage this arrangement, but mostly we don't. However, we seem to have found a way to accept the imperfect habits of the other.

We chuckle with good natured bantering, like when he tells people I change the sheets in the middle of the night when he gets up to pee, and I relate that I was really meant to live in Switzerland where things are clean, squared away and punctuality is a way of life. When the train schedule says it will be leaving the station at 2:18 PM, you had best be in your seat. Granted, occasionally I have a meltdown, but those are brief and relatively spaced out. This is good. If they weren't, I would be looking for husband number three, and John would be searching for wife number four.

Arriving back at my car, we said our goodbyes to Dave, reiterated our invitation to come visit us, and threw our packs and poles into the back of Lucy. She was parked all alone, on the side lawn of a house about half a mile past the parking lot on Sherwood Drive. My GPS got us back to the center of Boiling Springs, and we parked in front of the city pool.

"Are you sure you don't want to go for a swim and shower here?" I asked Julie.

"No, I want to go through my pack and sort out what I'm going to need for the rest of the hike. I'm going to send a lot of things back with you, too. You can either wait til I get home or just drop them off on my front porch. Ryan or Missy can put them inside when they come to feed the dogs." (Ryan and Missy are Julie's son and daughter-in-law.)

"OK. I guess I forgot what a cat you are when it comes to swimming. You know, you don't have to put your face in the water. It would feel good just to paddle around."

In all the years I have known this woman, I have never seen her submerge her entire body into water. Granted, I haven't been swimming with her all that many times and sitting in a hot tub is not the place to be going underwater. Still, she seems to have an aversion to total immersion. Her usual excuse is because she is wearing contacts or doesn't want to mess up her hair. Today, the contact reason would work, but her hair, like mine, looked pretty much like shit. Getting it wet could only improve the situation. Oh well. She didn't want to swim. I did. That was that.

Because I am older and although I am still adjusting to this over sixty thing I still cringe when I see my wrinkles. However, the perks that come with aging are pretty good. Being cheap to begin with, I am enjoying these senior discounts. The price for an adult to swim at The Boiling Springs City Pool for the day is twelve dollars. Can you believe that?? Twelve dollars to take a dip? Well, because I am a senior citizen, it is only five dollars. Excellent savings. Bottom line is that I would not have paid the twelve dollars. I would have driven home hot and smelly. No, I wouldn't have driven back to The Doyle to clean myself. I wasn't that smelly.

Hot damn! The water felt so good! This was another scorcher of a day, and there is nothing like a swimming pool to cool a body off. Showering afterward, even though the dressing room smelled faintly of urine, was still an experience of ecstasy. I found Julie back at Lucy, with her shit sprawled out all over the lawn, extending out a good ten feet.

"Jule, I'm hungry. How about if I go over to Anile's, where we had that good Italian dinner the other night and get us a couple of subs?

"That sounds great! I should be about finished sorting when you get back."

Just as I was getting into Lucy, Julie's phone rang. It was Janice inviting us to dinner and to spend the night, so Julie wouldn't have to stay in The Doyle. That was just so kind of her and Dave. I suspect that when he got home and told Janice what we had reported about the state of the rooms, they felt the need to provide an appropriate alternative. However, we both agreed to decline their very generous invitation. Julie really did want the experience, and I wanted to get home.

We sat at the edge of the lake, dangling our legs, enjoying the last meal of our adventure. I fed the ducks that quacked by and demanded their share. They were clearly accustomed to getting handouts. Then, we loaded up Julie's newly organized pack, I crammed the boxes to take home into the back, and we pointed Lucy toward Duncannon. Driving back to The Doyle, we talked about the past eight days. It seemed like so very long ago that we were talking to Boxer Brief, cramming our packs into the back of the rusty pickup at Pine Grove Furnace, and sitting on the patio of Dave and Janice's cabin. One hundred and ninety-two hours had passed by so quickly. Less than one brief second in the geologic time table, but crammed with memories so vivid, that they would be forever a source of comfort and a place of peace for the both of us.

When the hot flashes would once again wake us up in the middle of the night, which we knew all too well would be happening, we could go back to the trail in our heads. If that didn't make us tired enough to fall back to sleep, at least we wouldn't be stressing about the things we didn't get done the day before, and very likely wouldn't complete in the weeks ahead. Hey, when we found ourselves in boring, tedious situations, we could hit the trail. We would just have to know when to get off, because we still needed to pay the bills.

We hugged, like we did the time we arrived on our mountain bikes at the Massachusetts border, and when we got back home after riding those same mountain bikes 450 plus miles around the Gaspe Peninsula. There were no tears shed, but it was an emotional moment for us.

I know that hiking for eight days on the Appalachian Trail is no big deal, but it sure was for me. It served as a reminder that the old saying, "you are as old as you feel," really does mean exactly that. Just because I filed for social security and joined the ranks of the retired did not mean there weren't some adventures left for me to have.

Driving home, I entered my alternate world of living vicariously through the characters in my latest audio book, *Outlander*. I do most of my reading through audio books because I spend so much time in my car. Plus, for me, reading is sometimes like a sleeping pill, and after two pages, I nod off. There would be precious few books to my credit if I depended upon the printed page. This current book kept me wide awake on the road and riveted. While I listen to actress Davina Porter read with her very excellent Scottish brogue and English accent, doing all of the voices, I find myself in 18th century Scotland, with characters who now seem like friends. I want to keep up with their lives. I am transported, except that I really am on the interstate, in twenty-first century Pennsylvania.

I did not tell John I was coming home that day. My original plan stretched to ten days, but when I looked at the trail guide and searched for places to get off the trail should I decide to hike for another couple of days, there really wasn't an easy off place. It isn't like you can just walk for ten miles and call it a day, call for a ride, and head back to town. There are stretches where the trailheads are somewhat difficult to access.

When I was actually plodding along, planting my poles, cursing silently at the steep sections and not feeling that well, I thought of all the amenities of home and how good a shower would feel, how comfortable my bed would be, how easy to just turn on the cold water for a drink, and how nice to not be lugging my house around on my back. Even though I realized at the time that this was a unique experience, that replicating it might never happen, I still looked forward to the end of each day, when we got off the trail. I struggled with living in the moment, in the woods, with only the sounds of nature, save for the occasional hiker who passed us. And yes, they all seemed to pass us. Perhaps Julie kept up a better cadence when she was alone, but with me along, there was one speed, and it was first gear.

Now that the trail lay behind me, my mind drifted back to those long, hot, dusty, sweaty, tiring days, and I found myself missing it. I even missed the rocks and the hills. I missed being smelly and not caring that I was. I missed the freeze dried dinners and the fresh cold water we filtered from the many streams we crossed. I might add, that never, have I tasted water that good.

Although my thoughts meandered between Scotland, the trail, and getting home, I must say, I was feeling like I was in a very good place. I now know that I could have gone farther if I had wanted and that just because I have nearly sixty-two years behind me, didn't mean my hiking was finished. I was perhaps just getting started. Even if I never saw another blaze, I knew that I could, anytime I wanted.

I can't say that I wasn't glad to get home, to see my husband, to enjoy the amenities we all take for granted. I was very glad. Driving up the last hill, I gave a beep of the horn, rounded the corner and skidded to a halt. John was in the yard, puttering around, shadowed like always by Patrick Wiener Dog and Maxie Cat. Recognizing the car, Patrick bounded over, yelping, jumping, and running in circles. Maxie was a little more subtle with his greeting, but he was right there as well. I hugged my husband, gave him a quick peck on the cheek, and announced, "I'm back!"

But like all other trips I have ever been on, no matter how long I'm gone, when I walk through the front door, it feels like I never left. But this time, I returned with more than just my hiking gear and some dirty laundry. I came back with the additional and very welcomed baggage of my lost spirit.

Epilogue

It has been a couple of months since the experience of my Appalachian Trail hike. I enjoyed the rest of my summer, and I took gleeful pleasure in rolling over in bed on the day after Labor Day, the day I would have gone back to work, had I not retired. I am still trying things out, looking for a new *normal*. I still haven't developed a daily routine, and I need to do that, because I am a creature of habit. Most days I go to bed too late and sleep longer than I probably should. I suspect that will change, but right now, I'm content with floundering a bit. At least I do still go to our local YMCA each day as I have done for the past fifteen years. If I don't make it to the Y, I take a walk. I do something physical, partly because it feels good, partly because I know I should, partly because I still can. I still fret about my wrinkles, but my level of acceptance of them has improved. Slightly.

Julie and I are in contact most weeks, although we don't often cross paths. She is busy with her new roles as divorced woman, school nurse, B&B owner, and caring for Ruthie, who is an eighty-four year old mentally retarded firecracker. Julie claims she keeps her balanced. Ruthie believes in Santa, the Easter Bunny, and creates very interesting knitted items. And she likes beer.

We didn't see much of each other during the fall, but at Christmas we made it a point to get together. Being retired, my schedule is way more forgiving than hers. Really, at this point in my life, I have no schedule, so I offered to drive up to her place. As I parked my car in front of her house, I noticed an Asian family unloading their suitcases next to the garage. Above the garage was an apartment that Julie rented out as an Air B&B. This was a new business for her, having just started at the beginning of September. It has so far proved to be very successful as she is booked nearly every weekend.

This family was talking, laughing, pointing to different things around the yard. The father smiled, and greeted me, as did the mother.

"Hi. Isn't it beautiful here?" said the man

"Oh, hi. Yes, it is," I answered, politely.

"Are you looking for Julie?" asked the man.

"Yes," I answered.

"I think she's inside. Are you her mother?" asked the very horrid, clearly blind, disgusting, revolting little man.

HER MOTHER????? REALLY??? Just when I was feeling better about my age, my wrinkles, sagging skin. WTF???!!!

Walking up onto the porch, the door opened, and Julie greeted me. Her sister, Brenda, and brother-in-law, Steve, were also there.

"Sandy, I'm so glad you could come up! Did you meet my B&B guests for the weekend? The guy and his wife were actually my first customers, and they're back with their family. Can you believe all the way from Philadelphia?"

"Yes. We met. I. Hate. Him." I stated, stone faced and emphatic.

"OMG! What happened? What did he say to you?" asked Julie, with a look of horror on her face.

"He asked me if I was YOUR MOTHER!!"

Yes. Total eruption of laughter. From all of us. What could I say? C'est la vie. I can still strap on a pack, climb a hill, and live my life. Age is just a number, and I have always been a poor study in math.

Acknowledgments

No one writes a book without help. Ever. In my own case, there have been many, many folks over the years who supported and encouraged my writing efforts. Starting with a high school English teacher who liked my "style." Then there was Joyce, the woman who hired me for my first nursing job, which was private duty in her home. She liked the way I inserted humor into the care notes and gave me a book about how to get published for my 24th birthday. My writing journey began there.

I want to thank my daughter, Jamie, who even encouraged me during those years of parental embarrassment, and my chief editor and college roomie, Nancy, who thought this was good enough for her book club. We will see how that goes. It's hard to find words to recognize Julie, my bestie, for all crazy, hair-brained adventures. God help the nursing home who gets the two of us!

But most of all, I want to thank my husband, John, for his unending patience as I plodded along and tied up our computer. He never wavered in his belief that I could do this. Not only has he been my rock for nearly three decades, but the gentle breeze beneath my often floppy wings.

Made in the USA
Monee, IL
22 July 2022